I've known Joey since he was a young boy. He ⸻ book that refocuses Christians back into disciple making. This book cannot be ignored and must be read by Christians of all stripes. After reading the truths in his book, I just wish I had another ninety years to be able to go and make disciples.

—Fr. Luis Candelaria
Ateneo de Manila University, Philippines

Without doubt, discipleship is the missing ingredient in Christianity today. In *The LEGO Principle* Joey Bonifacio gets us back to the basic building blocks for making disciples. Joey is a leading practitioner in discipleship, as his church in the Philippines so powerfully demonstrates. This book could spark a revolution.

—Mark Conner
CityLife Church, Melbourne, Australia

The first time I met Joey Bonifacio was at a conference. He instantly won my trust and that of my Russian colleagues. Inspired by his message, one of our pastors moved to Manila for a six-month internship. The message of this book is virally winning the trust of thousands of young leaders around the globe.

—Lance Corley
International Teams, Moscow

After twenty-five years of publishing Christian literature, I have read countless manuscripts and books. Joey Bonifacio's *The LEGO Principle* was something unexpected. It's rich, inspiring, and life changing, so much so that I read it twice. If you only read one book this year—make sure it's this one.

—Keith Danby
International Bible Society, London

Who would ever think that the simple LEGO blocks could be the inspiration for a book on discipling and leaders? LEGOs—small, simple pieces of plastic for making connections for simple and/or intricate things. The LEGO Principle, simple but for making connections by and with people. Read this book to see how "simple" this is!

—John Dettoni
Chrysalis Ministries, San Clemente, California

I am thankful that my friend Joey Bonifacio has taken one of the main messages of his life and has put it into a well-researched, biblical, and easy-to-understand book. *The LEGO Principle* is based on many years of practical disciple making that I have seen work in Japan and all over the world. Make sure you read this book!

—SCOTT DOUMA
GRACE BIBLE CHURCH, YOKOHAMA, JAPAN

Joey Bonifacio has a knack of combining simplicity with depth. In *The LEGO Principle* he brings to life the power of discipleship and relationship. He is not merely theorizing because he lives the truth of his book every day. It is engrained in the church he leads. The church in America would do well to learn form him.

—BRYAN DWYER
ALPINE CHURCH, SALT LAKE CITY, UTAH

"Discipleship is relationship" is the life-changing truth Joey taught us in a London pub. It has shaped our ministry ever since. *The LEGO Principle* skillfully articulates the essential building blocks for the world-changing mission Christ has called us to. Armed with this truth, the potential of Christianity is limitless!

—WOLFI ECKLEBEN
EVERY NATION CHURCH, LONDON

The LEGO Principle is a good reminder to all Christians that discipleship is not the work of a few career ministers but the responsibility of every single believer. Fresh. Intelligent. Intuitive. Simple. Precise and practical as LEGO itself. I love this book.

—DARRELL GREEN
PRO FOOTBALL HALL OF FAME, WASHINGTON DC

The LEGO Principle is a practical and theologically accurate tool for all Christians. Joey is a man who has practiced and proven the principles of building and multiplying disciples in one of the largest churches in the world. The clear message of this book is anyone can make disciples and everyone should.

—JOEL HUNTER
NORTHLAND: A CHURCH DISTRIBUTED, LONGWOOD, FLORIDA

I first encountered Joey Bonifacio in his blog, "Discipleship Is Relationship." The concepts he has brought forth were not just out of the box but were also biblical and proven in day-to-day church life. *The LEGO Principle* shows Christians a simple way to face complex challenges in discipleship without being simplistic.

—DAVID LIM
LAUSANNE CONGRESS, MANILA

Every so often a book comes along that grows from the soul of an author who lives his message, who writes from the core of who he is, what he knows, and what he has accomplished. Joey Bonifacio is this kind of author. *The LEGO Principle* is this kind of book. Let the words of this rising global leader change the way you live.

—STEPHEN MANSFIELD
NEW YORK TIMES BEST-SELLING AUTHOR
THE MANSFIELD GROUP, WASHINGTON DC

The LEGO Principle taps into the most beautiful of all the basics of our faith. It reminds us that in Jesus we never grow beyond the basics; we just go deeper and stronger. Joey Bonifacio calls us back to the "beautiful basics" that invites us to a deep renewal of love for Jesus's way. I love this book!

—FLOYD MCCLUNG
ALL NATIONS, CAPE TOWN, SOUTH AFRICA

My very good friend and a leader I look to, Joey Bonifacio rocks. He is the real deal. His greatest strength is in raising disciples and leaders who are secure in their relationship with Jesus. His book *The LEGO Principle* will inspire you to enjoy connecting to God and with one another. A voice to a generation, you must read this book

—RACHEL ONG
MANAGING PARTNER, ROHEI, SINGAPORE

In *The LEGO Principle* Joey Bonifacio shows us a better way to build genuine connections. Read this book to discover how a crowd turns into a church that produces genuine New Testament disciples who make a difference in their community and our world.

—LARRY OSBORNE
NORTH COAST CHURCH, SAN DIEGO

The LEGO Principle is rooted in the nitty-gritty day-to-day living out of Christianity in the local church. More importantly it is deeply rooted in the truth of Scripture. Joey Bonifacio has written an important book for our times. Read it and be challenged to serve Jesus by making disciples.

—DARRIN PATRICK
ACTS 29 NETWORK, ST. LOUIS

What an enjoyable and beneficial read. Theologically solid. Insightful. Practical. Inspiring. As I read *The LEGO Principle*, I found myself wanting others I care about to read it as well. Do yourself a favor and read this book, then go and follow the practical convictions you will find in it.

—RANDY POPE
PERIMETER CHURCH, ATLANTA

The LEGO Principle will help Christians in the pews be disciples who makes disciples. It is an important book that will shape the future of the ministry of making disciples. Joey is not just its author; he is a living example of his book. He is also my friend, coach, and a vital consultant on church growth through discipleship.

—MARK RAMSEY
CITIPOINTE, BRISBANE, AUSTRALIA

For over seventeen years Joey has shared with me many simple yet profound nuggets of truth about discipleship. In *The LEGO Principle* he makes it available for all to read. From these truths their church Victory has grown from a few to tens of thousands and is today one of the world's fastest-growing churches.

—GORDON ROBERTSON
CHRISTIAN BROADCASTING NETWORK, VIRGINIA BEACH, VIRGINIA

Joey Bonifacio's delightful book *The LEGO Principle* answers two questions in relationship to the church. Our business? Discipleship. How's business? Not so great. This book is destined to change the future of discipleship. As a result it will change the direction of churches and impact our world.

—HAROLD J. SALA, PhD
GUIDELINES INTERNATIONAL MINISTRIES, LAGUNA HILLS, CALIFORNIA

Even though I'm a Catholic leader, when it comes to discipleship and church growth, Joey Bonifacio is my mentor. The many times we had coffee together were turning points in my ministry. The man walks his talk. *The LEGO Principle* contains Joey's life message. Read it and change the way you impact others forever.

—Bo Sanchez
Kerygma Magazine, Manila

Not only will you have a hard time putting down *The LEGO Principle*, its message resonates with the truth of God's Word that my friend Joey Bonifacio brings to life. It will again make the church what it should be—a place of loving, trusting, and caring relationships that reaches out and turns people into disciples of Jesus.

—Dirkie van der Spuy
Moreleta Park Association, Pretoria, South Africa

Relationships are central to making disciples as commanded by the Great Commission. Joey Bonifacio connects relationships to disciple making in a way that is sure to benefit all who read this book.

—Ed Stetzer
LifeWay Research, Nashville

The LEGO Principle is amazingly easy to grasp. Joey is clearly a man who loves making disciples, and his church is living proof of the eternal truth and effectiveness of what he writes. This book is as theologically sound as any book can get and yet is vitally relevant to the postmodern world we live in.

—Larry Stocktill
Bethany World Prayer Center, Baton Rouge, Louisiana

I have had the privilege of hearing the message of this book on several occasions when Joey Bonifacio visited China—it is always refreshing and at the same time convicting. Each time I hear it, I am reminded of the many times I spent with this man. This is not a message but a way of life.

—Steve
China

The LEGO Principle provides clear biblical strategies rooted in the Scriptures. As a thoughtful practitioner Joey provides us with clear insights that I urge all followers of Jesus to embrace. You will have a hard time putting down *The LEGO Principle*; it will capture your heart and change your life.

—Dr. Geoff Tunnicliffe
World Evangelical Alliance, New York

Build Relationships

Value People

Make Disciples

Change the World

The LEGO® Principle

THE POWER OF CONNECTING TO GOD AND ONE ANOTHER

JOEY BONIFACIO

CHARISMA
HOUSE

Most CHARISMA HOUSE BOOK GROUP products are available at special quantity discounts for bulk purchase for sales promotions, premiums, fund-raising, and educational needs. For details, write Charisma House Book Group, 600 Rinehart Road, Lake Mary, Florida 32746, or telephone (407) 333-0600.

THE LEGO PRINCIPLE by Joey Bonifacio
Published by Charisma House
Charisma Media/Charisma House Book Group
600 Rinehart Road
Lake Mary, Florida 32746
www.charismahouse.com

Unless otherwise noted, all Scripture quotations are from the Holy Bible, New International Version. Copyright © 1973, 1978, 1984, International Bible Society. Used by permission.

Scripture quotations marked ASV are from the American Standard Bible.

Scripture quotations marked ESV are from the Holy Bible, English Standard Version. Copyright © 2001 by Crossway Bibles, a division of Good News Publishers. Used by permission.

Scripture quotations marked KJV are from the King James Version of the Bible.

Cover design by Studio Gearbox
Design Director: Bill Johnson

Visit the author's website at www.joeybonifacio.com.

Library of Congress Cataloging-in-Publication Data:

Bonifacio, Joey.
  The LEGO principle / Joey Bonifacio. -- 1st ed.
      p. cm.
  Includes bibliographical references.
  ISBN 978-1-61638-677-1 (trade paper) -- ISBN 978-1-61638-678-8
(e-book)
  1. Discipling (Christianity) I. Title.
    BV4520.B58 2012
    269'.2--dc23
                              2012020524

First edition

12 13 14 15 16 — 9 8 7 6 5 4 3 2 1
Printed in the United States of America

To Jesus—this book is dedicated to You.

CONTENTS

INTRODUCTION

IT WAS 1988 when I bought my first two LEGO kits, the airport and the police station. I was a young father, excited to give my two young boys their Christmas presents. I had snuck the conspicuous boxes into the house and stashed them on the highest shelf in my bedroom cabinet far away from the boys' prying eyes and arms. To be sure they didn't discover the boxes, I camouflaged them with colored beach towels until I would wrap them late that night.

Since that time LEGO has become a part of our family's birthdays and celebrations. When my third son came along, my wife and I had the good sense to start him out with DUPLO, the larger bricks made for younger kids that he couldn't swallow even if he tried. In time all three of my boys would consider LEGO one of their all-time favorite toys. Over the years their LEGO toys have proved to be enduring and timeless.

This book, however, is not about the history of my children's playthings. It is about what Jesus said were the two most important commandments of all time: "'Love the Lord your God with all your heart and with all your soul and with all your mind and with all your strength.' The second is this: 'Love your neighbor as yourself.' There is no commandment greater than these."[1]

Jesus was making something clear to His listeners then as He is now: in life, it all boils down to loving God and loving one another. To put it another way, life is all about relationships—a relationship with God and then with one another.

This is why the title of this book is *The LEGO Principle*. You see, regardless of the shape, size, or color of a LEGO piece, each one is designed to do one thing: connect. LEGO pieces are designed to connect at the top and at the bottom. Like LEGO if you can connect to the top with God and to the bottom with others, you can pretty much shape the world you live in. And like LEGO, when the connections happen, the possibilities are limitless.

The years have whizzed by, and now my sons are adults; two of them have moved out of the house. While the boys and their LEGO toys are gone, what remain are the connections built through the years: the valuable, irreplaceable relationships that each of us has with God and with one another.

It is my sincere hope and prayer that this book will inspire you to live a life of wonderful, valuable connections. This, after all, is what Jesus taught His disciples.

SECTION I
DISCIPLESHIP

1.

JUST LIKE LEGO

THE STORY OF LEGO cannot be told without the account of its amazing founder, Ole Kirk Christiansen, a carpenter who lived in the town of Billund in Denmark. He started his trade by making household products from wood. In 1924 when his two sons, Godtfred and Karl, tried to light their oven at home, they ended up burning down the family home and the whole business with it. Flammable wood inventories and playful children don't mix very well. Thankfully the children were saved, but Ole Kirk's commercial future looked bleak.[1]

In less than a decade twin tragedies would pay the carpenter another visit. In 1932, as the Great Depression worsened in the United States, not even far-flung Billund and Ole Kirk's business would be spared by the crisis. Christian Humberg wrote in his book *50 Years of the LEGO Brick* that Ole Kirk "had to let his last employees go. His wife died soon afterward, the carpenter was left on his own, with four sons and not nearly enough orders."[2]

Jonathan Bender, author of *LEGO: A Love Story*, writes of the same adversities the carpenter encountered:

> At forty-one years of age, he was a widower living in the largest house in Billund, Denmark—a house that he soon might not be able to afford. The Great Depression meant that demand had dried up for stools, Christmas tree bases, and ironing boards that were the trademarks of his carpentry and joinery shop.[3]

But like many success stories these challenges would prove to be serendipitous. It was also in 1932 when Ole Kirk made the decision to manufacture wooden toys. Daniel Lipkowitz, author of *The LEGO Book: The Amazing LEGO Story*, writes:

> In 1932, with the worldwide Great Depression threatening to close his carpentry shop for good, Ole Kirk turned his skills to creating a range of toys for children. These beautifully made playthings included yo-yos, wooden blocks, pull-along animals, and vehicles of all kinds.[4]

His best seller was a pull-along wooden duck. "Ole Kirk guessed that even in times of financial strife, people would still be willing to buy wooden toys for their children."[5] In a matter of a few years business was good again, and Ole was able to build a new factory. More significantly this initial foray into toy manufacturing would become his family's core business more than fifty years later.

Yet in 1942 misfortune struck again. Another fire burned down the new factory, and "all the production patterns were lost."[6] At the same time Europe was facing an escalating world war. Both home products and toys were not in demand, and Ole Kirk's business wearily trudged through those years.

However, five years later serendipity would once again bring about a historical discovery. Humberg writes, "After the Second World War, high quality wood was in short supply, and plastic gradually began to dominate the world market."[7] With very little money he "finally took action; in 1947, Ole Kirk was the first Danish toy manufacturer to buy a plastic injection moulding machine—with borrowed money."[8] With Ole Kirk's newly acquired experience with plastics, the toy company soon would design, manufacture, and perfect the LEGO brick.

A CHRISTIAN HERITAGE

For years Ole Kirk experienced financial as well as other difficulties before his real breakthrough came. Only one thing would keep him going—his faith. Unknown to many, Ole Kirk Christiansen, the founder of LEGO, was a follower of Christ.

In their book *The Ultimate LEGO Book* authors David Pickering, Nick Turpin, and Caryn Jenner wrote that Ole Kirk's faith helped him through personal crises, including the death of his wife in 1932, which left him with four young sons to look after.[9] He and his family were members of a Danish Christian movement called Indre Mission, and even into the 1950s, when the LEGO company was still a small business, almost everyone would meet together for a short prayer before work.[10,11]

Jonathan Bender, alluding to the years in 1932 when Ole Kirk's problems were at their worst, writes of how he responded to those challenges as a Christian:

> That year, Ole Kirk's life was at a crossroads. His first wife, Kirstine, had died giving birth to their fourth son, Gerhardt. "Life is a gift, but also a challenge," Ole Kirk, a devout Christian, is said to have remarked around that time.[12]

The fact that Ole Kirk Christiansen was a Christian is incidental to why this book is titled *The LEGO Principle*. It is, however, a good story to know. This book is titled as such because it is all about connecting—connecting to God and connecting to others. It is what Jesus and the Bible often describe as becoming a disciple or a follower of Christ.

Open any LEGO box, and you'll find a variety of colors, shapes, and sizes. There are red, blue, green, brown, yellow, orange, white, black, gray, and other color pieces. There are fat, flat, rectangular, round, square, thick, thin, long, and short pieces.

Though there is a wide assortment of LEGO pieces, they are all designed to do one thing: *connect*. To connect means to attach, to associate, and to bond. LEGO bricks and pieces are designed with studs on top that interlock with the bottom of each piece. While LEGO bricks are so varied, they all have one purpose: to connect at the top and at the bottom.

Just like LEGO pieces that connect at the top and at the bottom, discipleship is about connecting to God and with one another. This is the LEGO Principle: *Connect first to God and then to one another.*

It does not matter what one's skin color, social background, age, or denomination is—God designed us all to connect to Him and then to one another. Jesus said the foremost commandment is about connecting with God: "'Love the Lord your God with all your heart and with all your soul and with all your mind.' This is the first and greatest commandment."[13] Then He said, "The second is like it: 'Love your neighbor as yourself.'"[14]

These two commandments combine to become the LEGO Principle: Connect to God. Connect to one another. This to Jesus was what it meant to be His disciple.

A "FOLLOWER"

Mathetes is the Bible's Greek word for disciple. It primarily meant to be a pupil or a student. But unlike our present-day meaning of the words *pupil* and *student*, which we tend to think of as one who goes to school to learn a subject such as algebra or biology, the word *disciple* had a much deeper meaning in Jesus's day. It meant to be a follower of someone's teaching.

Thus the word *disciple* meant someone who closely followed a teacher and had a relationship with that person. It literally meant the sharing of life lessons that were fully intended to be lived out in day-to-day life. More than just learning in a class, to be a disciple meant to have a relationship with the teacher. Jesus took this popular cultural practice of His time and used it as the basis to connect us to God and to one another.

Similarly the word *follower* today means something completely different than it did back then. Depending on what part of the world you come from, a follower can mean anything and everything from a blind adherent to a groupie or someone who lives on other people's tweets.

LIKE A JOURNEY

Discipleship pundit Bill Hull writes, "*Ship* added to the end of *disciple* means 'the state of' or 'contained in.' So *discipleship* means the state of being a disciple. In fact, the term *discipleship* has a nice ongoing feel—a sense of journey, the idea of becoming a disciple rather than having been made a disciple."[15]

Thus the word *discipleship* meant to follow God while being contained in a lifelong journey of faith with Jesus and His other followers—to connect to God and to one another. In Matthew Jesus explains the essence of this journey.

Therefore go and *make disciples* of all nations, *baptizing* them in the name of the Father and of the Son and of the Holy Spirit, *and teaching* them to obey everything I have commanded you. And surely I am with you always, to the very end of the age.[16]

According to Jesus, making disciples or discipleship involves two things:

- Baptizing people in the name of the Father, Son, and Holy Spirit

- Teaching them to obey everything He commanded

First, let's take a closer look at what it means to baptize people in the name of the Father, Son, and Holy Spirit. Part of the problem in defining baptism is that, depending on one's Christian background and denomination, it can take on a variety of meanings. To avoid going into a long dissertation on what the sacrament of baptism is, allow me to go straight to the heart and spirit of the practice. The best way to do that is to see what baptism meant to Jesus.

Immersed into a divine relationship

In Matthew 3:15 we see how Jesus went out of His way to be baptized by His cousin John. His reason: "It is proper for us to do this to fulfill all righteousness." When He was baptized He was immersed, submerged, and soaked. Every part of Him was dedicated and consecrated as He publicly identified Himself with God.

What was more significant was not the actual ritual but the result of Jesus's baptism. The following passage tells us what happened:

As soon as Jesus was baptized, he went up out of the water. At that moment heaven was opened, and he saw the Spirit of God descending like a dove and lighting on him. And a voice from heaven said, "This is my Son, whom I love; with him I am well pleased."[17]

Here we find a picture of what baptism is to Jesus: to be immersed into the fellowship of the Father, Son, and Holy Spirit. Author Rick Warren explains this relationship in his book *The Purpose Driven Life*:

> [God's] very nature is relational, and he identifies himself in family terms: Father, Son, and Spirit. The Trinity is God's relationship to himself.[18]

In Jesus's baptism we see that being a disciple is all about immersing oneself into a divine relationship. To us it is an open invitation to become a part of this relationship, eternity's very first "small group"—a relationship with the Father, Son, and Holy Spirit. At the end of the day discipleship is a journey into a relationship with God and His people.

Immersed into the family of God

Jesus further said that we were to be baptized or immersed into the name of the Father, Son, and Holy Spirit. In biblical times a person's name described his identity and character, and still today it denotes one's heritage and ancestry—his family. Thus to be baptized in the name of the Father, Son, and Holy Spirit is to be immersed into the identity, character, and family of God.

Although I don't believe it is necessary for one to be baptized in the ocean, it paints a good picture of baptism. It brings to light the reality of how infinitely big God is and how small we are, that we are unable to contain God and instead every part of us is to be immersed, soaked, and saturated by Him.

To be Jesus's disciple is to be immersed in a relationship with the Trinity. It came at the cost of one of its members giving His life so we could become a part of the family. Discipleship is relationship. David Platt emphasizes the same thought in his book *Radical*:

> Disciple making is not about a program or an event but about a relationship. As we share the gospel, we impart life, and this is the essence of making disciples. Sharing the life of Christ. This is why making disciples is not just about going, but it also includes baptizing.[19]

THE SECOND HALF OF THE DEFINITION

According to Jesus, the second half of discipleship is "teaching them to obey everything that I have commanded."[20] Undoubtedly, teaching is a vital component of discipleship. However, more than just teaching, Jesus's real emphasis is obedience. He said, "Teaching them *to obey* everything I have commanded." And what did Jesus mean by obeying His command? He said, "If you love me, you will obey what I command."[21]

Isn't it amazing how we see obedience to God's commands as following rules while Jesus sees them from the standpoint of a relationship? And what was one of Jesus's foremost commands? "This is my command: Love each other."[22]

To Jesus, obeying His commands meant loving one another. Discipleship is relationship. He also said, "You are my friends if you do what I command."[23] To Jesus, obeying His commands was all about relationship. And how will the world know that we are Jesus's disciples? "All men will know that you are my disciples, if you love one another."[24]

The world will know that we are His disciples by the quality of our relationship with Him and with one another.

NOT ENOUGH TO JUST KNOW

What makes Christianity unique among all other religions is it teaches people how to grow in their relationship with God and with others. The goal of teaching is not merely to increase our knowledge of divine principles, rules, laws, and things to do but to grow in our relationship with God and one another.

If discipleship is just learning more without deepening our relationship with God and one another, then we run the risk of being rebuked by Jesus, just as He did the religious people of His day when He said:

> You diligently study the Scriptures because you think that by them you possess eternal life. These are the Scriptures that testify about me, yet you refuse to come to me to have life.[25]

In today's language it might have sounded like this, "You keep going to your Bible studies and meetings, thinking that by doing so you're getting closer to Me. Yet you resist living a life in relationship with Me." The idea behind all the teaching and learning is that the deepening of our understanding of God will result in a stronger and deeper relationship with Him. John Wesley warned about learning and not growing in relationship: "Beware you be not swallowed up in books! An ounce of love is worth a pound of knowledge."[26]

Peter was one of Jesus's closest disciples. He was also one of the first of His disciples to publicly deny his relationship with Jesus. What did Jesus ask Peter after he denied Him? "Do you love me?"[27]

Jesus did not ask him if he had been coming to church or how many Bible studies he had missed. He did not even confront him and say, "Why did you deny Me?" The question He asked Peter was simply, "Do you still love me?" Jesus knew love was more powerful than just being held accountable.

Clearly to Jesus discipleship is all about relationship. To Him the very foundation and basis of ministry to people is our relationship with Him. Notice what He told Peter after He asked him, "Do you love me?" He told him, "Feed my sheep."[28]

Our ability to love others and give of ourselves to people comes only as a fruit of our understanding and appreciation of our relationship with God. John tells us that: "We love because he first loved us."[29]

To Jesus, teaching was just the vehicle to help people learn how to love God and others. Relationship was the end goal, not teaching. Discipleship is relationship!

THE TEACHINGS OF PAUL

Next to Jesus the second most important teacher in the New Testament was the apostle Paul. Acts 18:11 tells us, "Paul stayed for a year and a half, teaching them the word of God." That time of teaching was spent in Corinth. In Paul's first letter to the Corinthians, we find that his teaching was no different from Jesus's. He warns us, "Knowledge puffs up, but love builds up."[30]

This profound seven-word admonition is another way of saying that knowledge by itself will make you arrogant and proud. The second half of the statement tells us what is better than just learning new things—love. Love and relationships are what builds up.

There is no doubt that Paul's foundational teaching in Corinth is about Christ and His cross. A central component of this focused on love and relationships. He taught that while you can learn to have the wisdom and the power of the Spirit, the real key is love. He writes, "And now I will show you the most excellent way."[31]

What to Paul was the most excellent way? Love. In the succeeding chapter he explains what love is. He exhorts the Corinthian church that love is preeminent over spiritual gifts and acts of service. Let me paraphrase Paul's words this way: "Great that you speak in tongues. Awesome when you can prophesy. Amazing that you are a deep thinker and can fathom the mysteries of life. Fantastic that you have faith that can move mountains. Wonderful that you take care of the poor. But if you don't have love, you really don't have anything."

He caps it by saying: "And now these three remain: faith, hope and love. But the greatest of these is love."[32] In his book *The Making of a Christian Leader*, the late Ted Engstrom can only agree with Paul's teaching:

> The Bible considers our relationship more important than our accomplishment. God will get His work done! He does not demand that we accomplish great things; He demands that we strive for excellence in our relationships.[33]

As a new Christian reading this in 1987, these three sentences transformed the way I read the Bible and how I lived out my faith in God. Discipleship is not a program. It is all about relationships, first with God then with others.

Paul, like Jesus, also taught the Corinthians that ministry is rooted in relationships.

> All this is from God, who reconciled us to himself through Christ and gave us the ministry of reconciliation: that God was reconciling the world to himself in Christ, not counting men's sins against them. And he has committed to us the message of reconciliation.[34]

In this passage Paul explains that ministry is all about reconciling people to God. Reconciliation is a theological term that primarily deals with relationships. Like Jesus, Paul taught that ministry is about restoring people into a relationship with God. As they grow in that relationship, they too will be reconciled to others.

Paul not only taught that his way of making disciples is rooted in relationships, he also demonstrated it. He told the Corinthians, "I am not writing this to shame you, but to warn you, as my dear children."[35]

In this verse we see how Paul admonished, adjusted, and held disciples accountable. He did it in the context of relationship as one does his own children. Paul's brand of teaching was not in set classes but in relationships. Later in the same letter Paul wrote, "Therefore I urge you to imitate me."[36]

More than just teaching them, he said, "Imitate me." To imitate someone means you have to be close to him. It is in up-close relationships that one can best be made into a disciple and make disciples. Francis Frangipane put it this way: "While the doctrines of Christianity can be taught, Christlikeness can only be inspired."[37]

AN UNFORGETTABLE REMINDER

In his letter to the Corinthians Paul dealt with the sacrament of Communion. When he taught on the topic, Paul merely passed on what Jesus had instructed:

> For I received from the Lord what I also passed on to you: The Lord Jesus, on the night he was betrayed, took bread, and when he had given thanks, he broke it and said, "This is my body, which is for you; do this in remembrance of me." In the same way, after supper he took the cup, saying, "This cup is the new covenant in my blood; do this, whenever you drink it, in remembrance of me."[38]

What was the instruction that Jesus and Paul left to the disciples? "Remember me." To remember means to not forget. Jesus was saying, "Don't forget what I did for you. It is the ultimate expression of My love for you."

In teaching the sacrament of Communion, Jesus and Paul instituted the simplest and most memorable of mnemonic devices—the bread and the cup. Both are common things that we encounter daily when we eat. The devices were brilliant, timeless, and hard to forget.

The genius of it all is that people don't often forget to eat; they usually do so multiple times a day. Jesus knew that even when we forget Him, we would not forget to eat. This way every time we eat we can take a moment to be reminded of our relationship with the Father, Son, and Holy Spirit. Every meal becomes an opportunity to partake of His grace and commune with Him, a reminder that we are sinners saved by grace. As such we have the divine privilege of having a relationship with Him.

A few years ago I was asked to teach church leaders in China about discipleship. Risking their lives to hear fresh insights on discipleship, people from all over the nation came. It was inspiring to see these precious saints so hungry to learn.

After three days of equipping leaders, the feedback was very positive. On the third day I realized it wasn't just a lesson to them. As the meeting drew to a close, the leaders administered Communion to the more than a hundred people who were there. Communion was not the typical ceremony of passing around itty-bitty elements, singing, and praying—all in about ten to fifteen minutes.

It was an extended thirty to forty minutes of sharing fist-sized pieces of bread and big Styrofoam cups filled with red juice. For a good ten minutes each person silently sat and recalled the love of Christ as He bore our sins in His broken body and spilled His blood to wash us clean. Many of them wept.

After this time of reflection, the people quietly walked to the other tables offering to pray. The prayer concerns ranged from persecution from family, friends, and the government to the more serious threat of being pregnant with a second child, as the one-child policy is still enforced in parts of China to this day.

After prayers and a time of encouragement, the people moved to another table and began to pray again. Some laughed, some wept, and some just talked and prayed. That day it became clear why they have received the message of "discipleship is relationship" so well. They live it.

It's no wonder the church in China continues to grow at breakneck speed. As the *London Times* reports: "Christianity in China is booming. With 100 million believers, far more than the 74 million-member communist party, Jesus is a force to be reckoned with in the People's Republic."[39]

The *Times'* estimate is not very far from that of other Christian organizations such as the US Center for World Missions. This current growth trend shows that China will soon surpass the United States to become the nation with the largest concentration of Christians.

What used to be church growth among the peasantry in outlying rural areas has now spread into China's cities. Hong Kong's *Sunday Morning Post* reports of a church that meets in the very capital of China, Beijing.

> Attended by a well-to-do and educated crowd—among them university lecturers, doctors, lawyers, NGO workers and even Communist Party members—Shouwang has come to symbolize a new breed of young urban Christians who are no longer contented to practice their faith in secret."[40]

This is the power of discipleship through relationships, and it works everywhere—in religious Manila, communist China, and metropolitan Manhattan.

Christians commonly say, "Christianity is not a religion, it is a relationship," and yet all too often behave otherwise. Just like LEGO bricks, our life is about connecting to the top with God and connecting with others. Discipleship is not about being converted and converting others, nor is it about cramming our heads with information about the Bible. It is about relationship, one that expresses itself in loving God and loving others. The primary reason we read the Bible is to know the God of the Bible.

Here's how Andy Stanley and Bill Willits put it in their book *Creating Community*:

"A curriculum or a series of classes may be helpful, but they shouldn't be considered the determinants for spiritual growth. They may help people become better informed about their faith, but they don't automatically lead people to maturity.... At the risk of oversimplifying, it seems clear that Jesus is saying that loving God and loving your neighbor is what it all comes down to....These two activities give evidence of a person's spiritual growth and maturity."[41]

2.

IN ONE WORD

TEN MINUTES TO go. There I was sitting on the stage waiting for my turn to speak before a distinguished audience of bishops, seminary professors, church leaders, and theologians. It was tense. I was intimidated.

I had spoken before large audiences but none quite like this one. These leaders had planted, grown, and overseen hundreds if not thousands of churches. And here I was, a pastor of one congregation, a guest speaker. How did I get myself into this?

Two weeks before the event, despite the written invitation, the website, and the bulletin with my name on it, I still could not believe I was chosen to speak to this group of leaders on the topic of discipleship. I called the man who invited me, David Lim, director of the Lausanne Philippines Congress, to ask if he was sure he had the right person. I told him he might have mistaken me for Pastor Steve Murrell, the founder of our fellowship.

I was half hoping he would say, "Is he available to speak?" Instead he replied, "Send us your notes so we can print handouts for your sessions." Now I was not only going to be heard, but they also would have printed evidence of anything stupid I might say.

So there I was, under pressure, counting the minutes before my turn. Any speaker knows the importance of connecting with his audience in the first three to four minutes of a speech. That rapport is important and often determines the flow and eventual outcome of one's speech. But what could I say that would make these seasoned leaders responsive to the urgent business I wanted to bring to their attention?

A Last-Minute Idea

The man who spoke before me was preparing to end his session. In the last few minutes before my turn I had a flash of inspiration: *start with a game*. Immediately I scribbled brand names of different products on the back of the program. In the background I could hear the emcee read my bio. It was time.

I decided to begin my message with a "one word" game and asked for volunteers. I said, "I'm going to say a brand name or a popular trademark. I want you to answer, in only one word, the business the company represents."

It worked. I got their attention. It felt good as I watched some of them loosen up and get ready to participate. Even bishops like playing games.

"Are you ready?" I asked. Glancing at my list, the first trademark I called out was "Starbucks." Instantly someone replied, "Coffee." "Wow, you guys are amazing!" I encouraged.

By now I had them smiling. It was obvious they were enjoying the exercise. Next I called out, "Toyota." Immediately someone answered, "Cars." Then I said, "Rolex," and Dr. Lim himself responded, "Watches," without hesitation. Group participation was riding high as the crowd eagerly awaited the next trademark. I knew I had connected.

Then it was time to bring the point behind my game home. For my last example I said, "Church." And the room was silent. Minds were whirling, "Hmm, what is the 'business' of the church? What is the church's 'one word'?"

Since that day at the conference, I have done this exercise with other Christian leaders in Australia, Brazil, China, the United Kingdom, United States, and other places. Over time I have refined the game to include a PowerPoint presentation showing the actual logos and trademarks of various products.

Interestingly enough, everywhere I have played the "one word" game I received the same reaction as I did at the first conference. People immediately knew the businesses of each trademark with absolute certainty. Even more important, they could define it in one word. Yet without fail, every time I showed the last picture, usually the logo of their church, there would either be a stumped silence, sporadic whispers, or a variety of guesses.

In the words of astronaut John Swigert, "Houston, we have a problem." That was his way of telling his colleagues at NASA that the Apollo 13 space shuttle was off course. In saying this, I am not talking about the heart and motive of the church leaders I have talked with or the people attending the conferences and meetings. I am merely pointing out the obvious lack of clarity.

Why is it that companies such as Starbucks and Toyota can be described so simply in one word and the church is having a hard time figuring out what its "one word" is? And if church leaders are unsure of the one word, is it any wonder that Christians are just as unclear of what church is about?

You may be thinking, "What's the big deal about knowing one's 'one word' anyway?" The big deal is clarity. Clarity allows people to know exactly what to expect from an organization. No one who goes to Starbucks is expecting a pizza. The clearer the expectations, the easier it is for people to interface with the church at any level. Having a "one word" is all about keeping things clear and simple.

In their book *Simple Church* Thom Rainer and Eric Geiger explain the need for simplicity:

> Many of our churches have become cluttered. So cluttered that people have a difficult time encountering the simple and powerful message of Christ. So cluttered that many people are busy doing church instead of being the church.[1]

The question we should ask is, where did all this clutter come from? Surely it could not have come from Jesus. He was the epitome of simplicity. As Rainer and Geiger further point out, "If anyone knows simple, it is Jesus. He is the original simple revolutionary."[2]

They're right in their advice to keep things simple. After all, Jesus, who founded the church, was a carpenter's son, and His first followers were fishermen, men who the Bible says were ordinary and unschooled.[3] We can be certain Jesus led these men in very simple ways. Somehow over time we have managed to complicate what was meant to be simple.

Clearing away the clutter allows us to focus on the "one word." Zeroing in on the "one word" is all about focusing on one's purpose. This is why a discussion on the "one word" is important. It defines, clarifies, and focuses one's purpose.

What is our "one word" as Christians? This brings us back to the Gospel of Matthew, where Jesus's final words are clear and simple:

> Therefore go and make disciples of all nations, baptizing them in the name of the Father and of the Son and of the Holy Spirit, and teaching them to obey everything I have commanded you. And surely I am with you always, to the very end of the age.[4]

It doesn't get any clearer than that. There were a number of options Jesus could have given. He could have said, "Go and build strong marriages, go and raise healthy families, go and heal the sick, go and care for the poor, go be a raving success, or even go and plant churches." But He didn't. He said, "Go and make disciples."

Jesus came to earth for one reason and one purpose alone: to save us from our sins.[5] He also knew that the best way to communicate His life-changing message of salvation to a sinful world is through the personal experience and witness of individual people, His disciples.[6]

Without God We Can't; Without Us He Won't

There is a curious incident in the tenth chapter of the Book of Acts about a Roman centurion who feared the Lord but had not encountered the message of the gospel.

> One day at about three in the afternoon he had a vision. He distinctly saw an angel of God, who came to him and said, "Cornelius!"
>
> Cornelius stared at him in fear. "What is it, Lord?" he asked.
>
> The angel answered, "Your prayers and gifts to the poor have come up as a memorial offering before God. Now send men to Joppa to bring back a man named Simon who is called Peter. He is staying with Simon the tanner, whose house is by the sea."[7]

Several thoughts come to mind when I consider this passage. First, Cornelius was a God-fearing man who prayed, he was also generous, and yet he and his family still needed to hear the gospel preached to them. The second thought is, why would the angel have to leave a complicated set of instructions for Cornelius to find Peter instead of just giving the message himself? After all, he was already there. Why the tedious process?

LeRoy Eims, the former director of US Ministries for the discipleship organization The Navigators, explains why.

> The reason for the angel's not doing any of these things is rather simple. God does not use angels as His witnesses. He uses people. Just imagine what God could have done to get the Good News of Jesus Christ to a needy world. He could have put an angel into orbit broadcasting the gospel in every language. But He didn't. He chose to use people.[8]

God has ordained people to reach people. It is as the famous quote says, "Without God we can't; without us He won't."

Discipleship is God's strategy for transforming the world. When Christians insist on sidestepping the call to make disciples, we end up going around in circles rather than fulfilling our purpose on earth. Missiologist and my longtime ministry partner Jun Escosar puts it this way:

> God's intent was not just to make us saints who are heaven-bound. The word "saint(s)" is mentioned forty-five times in the Bible. Neither were we called to simply be believers of Jesus. Even the word "Christian" was used only three times in Scripture. On the other hand the words "disciple(s)" overwhelmingly show up more than 260 times in the New Testament.[9]

There is an urgent call for the people of God to return to this lost art of making disciples. We cannot keep avoiding discipleship and still say we have remained true to the Scriptures. If we are to put "one word" to the purpose of the church, I believe it must be "discipleship." There is no Plan B for reaching the world. There is only one plan—discipleship. Christians should stop dodging the word. It's time we fully embraced it. Discipleship is, after all, the very "business" of the church.

REAL CONSEQUENCES

The consequences are inconsequential when Starbucks defocuses from coffee to teas and Frappuccinos, or when Toyota manufactures outboard motors. But when the church is unable to carry out what it was created to do, the repercussions are catastrophic.

Here is the Gallup organization's Albert Winseman on the current state of churches in the United States:

> Let me say it again: the Church in the United States is in serious trouble. All the warning signs are there. Some more obvious than others. One ominous sign is that congregational membership as a proportion of the U.S. population is shrinking....Church membership growth is not keeping up with population growth; the Church is losing ground....
>
> For example, in 1968, there were 11 million United Methodists in the United States attending 42,000 churches. By 2003, there were 8.1 million members in almost 35,000 churches. That's a drop-off during those 35 years of 26% in membership and 17% in the number of congregations.
>
> For the Presbyterian Church (USA), the news is worse: In the same time frame, it has gone from 4 million members in 12,000 churches to 2.4 million members in 11,000 churches—a decline of 40% in membership and 8% in the number of congregations.
>
> But the decline is hardly limited to mainline Protestants. Gallup Organization polling data show that the percentage of Americans who identify themselves as Southern Baptists has declined by more than half in the past decade: from 10% in 1995 to 4% in 2005.[10]

Even the bright spots are not so bright. Winseman goes on to say that despite the growth of megachurches in the last two decades, the percentage of Christians in the United States who choose not to affiliate with a denomination has remained steady. So instead of actually growing, the church is seeing "a reshuffling of the deck chairs on that famous, iceberg-bound ship."[11]

What's more, the problem is not limited to Protestants. Winseman writes, "Roman Catholics are in the midst of a severe shortage of priests that doesn't show signs of abating—and this was a crisis even before the sexual abuse scandals of the last few years broke into the news."[12]

Could this current decline of the church in the United States be due to the fact that it has strayed from its "one word," or its purpose for existing? According to The Barna Group, the root of the problem is the church's lack of discipleship.

> Despite pockets of progress, many wonderful local stories and several dependable models, the American church as a whole is still failing in the very thing Jesus emphasized most in His final words on earth: making disciples.
>
> Don't believe it? Here's a snapshot of the fruit of our discipleship efforts:
>
> - Seven out of 10 born-again Christians don't believe in moral absolutes, while only 10 percent base their moral decision-making on the principles taught in the Bible.
> - 59 percent of Christians believe that Satan isn't an actual being but simply a symbol of evil, while 58 percent say the Holy Spirit is merely a symbol of God's power or presence. Another 39 percent think Jesus sinned while on earth.
> - 61 percent of twenty-somethings who had been active in a church youth group are now spiritually disengaged, while only one-fifth remained as spiritually active as during their school years.[13]

Author Bill Hull has consistently sounded the alarm on the need for discipleship and the cost of sidestepping this most fundamental Christian practice, our "one word." He writes: "Still many resist Jesus' call to discipleship. We've been taught that discipleship is optional or that it only involves establishing new believers. The cost to God's kingdom that our resistance has caused is incalculable and inexcusable."[14]

As I pointed out earlier, the Greek word translated *disciple* simply means someone who is a follower. Therefore to make disciples means to draw people first to Christ then to show them how to follow Him in hopes of seeing them become Christlike.

Describing C. S. Lewis's thoughts on following Jesus and the role of the church, author Will Vaus writes: "This gets to the heart of the church's purpose. Lewis saw that purpose to be: drawing people to Christ and making them like Christ. He said that the church exists for no other purpose."[15]

Lewis himself explained in very strong terms how vital this role is. "If the Church is not doing this," he said, "then all the cathedrals, clergy, missions, sermons, even the Bible, are a waste of time."[16] Discipleship is the very purpose of the church. It is our "one word," the one business we should focus on and attend to.

While Bill Hull has expressed the "incalculable and inexcusable" results of our lack of discipleship, he is positive that the situation is not irreversible.

> The cost to God's kingdom that our resistance has caused is incalculable and inexcusable. Yet it's not unforgiveable or unchangeable. We must change, and I'm happy to say that transformational discipleship—the disciple making that Jesus taught and that his disciples practiced—is being restored to the church.[17]

Hull is right. In many places around the world God is restoring the heart of discipleship. This book is in line with Hull's call to return to the church's "one word," discipleship. But please don't think this is another treatise on models, definitions, and systems on discipleship. I ask that you please keep an open heart and an open mind. This book is not about methods, practices, and programs. It's about a realistic and practical way to disciple our friends, families, and cities one person at a time. More importantly, it's biblical.

This book also is not about advocating a simple solution for the myriad of complex issues mentioned above. By simplicity, I mean the church must focus on the one thing Christians should be busy with. There is nothing simple about man and his proclivity to sin. Discipleship is the simple answer; the art of making disciples is not quite that simple, hence this book.

DISCIPLESHIP, 7-ELEVEN, AND STARBUCKS

Apart from identifying a "one word" to rally around, we must also share the same understanding of its meaning. Having the same "one word" is pointless if we do not have the same definition. Different definitions lead to different practices and standards. It is one thing to know your "one word"; it's a totally different matter to explain it.

For example, what Starbucks calls coffee is completely different from 7-Eleven's version of the brew. There is a big difference between the coffee dispensed at 7-Eleven and the one served at Starbucks. They're not the same thing.

The difference stems from each company's "one word." 7-Eleven's goal is not to sell coffee but to sell convenience. It is the neighborhood store that can meet your immediate needs twenty-four hours daily. Coffee is not their one thing; convenience is.

Starbucks, on the other hand, is all about coffee. Every shelf is loaded with coffee or things about it. This is what Starbucks CEO Howard Schultz wrote about the first time he stepped inside the coffee shop:

> The minute the door opened, a heady aroma of coffee reached out and drew me in....Along another wall was an entire shelf full of coffee-related merchandise, including a display of Hammarsplast coffeemakers, in red, yellow, and black.[18]

From day one it was clear what the business was about: coffee. And though the idea is to make their stores the "third place" for people, next to their homes and workplaces, all that revolves around enjoying coffee.

As coffee is to 7-Eleven, so often is discipleship to churches. They take it on as a part of their purpose and not *the* reason for their existence. I have found that churches tend to place discipleship on their shelves the way 7-Eleven has only an area in their stores for coffee. Discipleship is not the main thing but one of many things. Thus, scores of Christians are aware of discipleship but have vastly different understandings of what it is.

Whether it's serving the community, reaching out to the poor, or simply growing a church, these purposes of the church were to be accomplished through discipleship. That was Jesus's original intent—for the work of the ministry to be done through discipleship and for discipleship to be achieved through relationships.

One Relationship at a Time

I credit Steve Murrell for my early understanding of discipleship as relationship. Steve was an American missionary to the Philippines when I met him. I can still remember the evening he invited my wife and me to their apartment in Manila for dinner more than twenty-five years ago. It would become one of the biggest turning points in my walk as a Christian.

Marie and I had never been invited for dinner at a pastor's home. Not knowing what to expect, we dressed in our Sunday best. I was decked in business attire, and Marie was dressed like she was meeting the pope. I did one last check at us then gingerly rang the doorbell. To our surprise as the door opened there was Steve in T-shirt, shorts, and barefoot with his six-month-old son tucked in his arm like a football.

The first thing that hit me was how real it all was. There was no façade, no "christianese," no veils. What struck me about Steve and Deborah was that they were normal people—people whom we could connect with, people whom we could be friends with. For some reason I never expected that from a pastor.

That evening Marie and I started a friendship with Steve and Deborah that has lasted more than two decades, a friendship that would impact every area of our lives—our faith, our family, our finances, and one day even our vocation. It is what I mentioned earlier, discipleship, a journey of faith with God and other followers of Christ, one relationship at a time.

The global advertising agency Saatchi & Saatchi lists LEGO among the top fifty most loved and respected brands in the world. It has become such a part of people's lives it is now an official word in the dictionary: LEGO /'legō/ noun. A construction toy consisting of interlocking plastic building blocks.[19]

The LEGO company has a unique "one word"—LEGO, the toy. It has managed to remove the clutter and focus on that one word. LEGO does not mean anything but LEGO. For more than fifty years it has been responsible for transforming the way people play, learn, and think. It manufactures a toy that is so simple yet capable of shaping things that are complex.

Similarly, discipleship is the Christian's "one word." It is the simple act of becoming a follower of Christ and helping others do the same in the context of a relationship. If we can connect to God and to one another, we can pretty much shape the world together.

3.

DISCIPLESHIP IS RELATIONSHIP

ONE OF THE reasons I like using LEGO to describe discipleship is it is a picture of quality enjoyment. I am reminded of the many happy hours my three sons spent playing with these toys. Even now that my children are adults, all I have to do is close my eyes, and I can see their happy faces and stubby fingers as they busily play with their LEGO pieces. A sense of joy fills me at the thought. I believe the delight my children experienced playing with their toys mirrors God's plan for us in discipleship.

Too often the word *discipleship* is linked with religious duty, increased commitment, or intense discipline. If we read carefully, we find that the overarching theme of the Bible is enjoying a relationship with God and with one another. Even the first book of the Bible, Genesis, introduces God's desire for relationship and enjoyment.

Have you ever wondered why God rested on the seventh day? Did He get tired from making all the giraffes and elephants in Africa? Was it the scores of creatures in the Amazon that did Him in? Or was it from making too many Asians like me? The prophet Isaiah tells us, "The Creator of the heavens and earth never gets tired or weary,"[1] which begs the question: If God does not get tired or weary, why did He rest on the seventh day?

I believe God rested on the seventh day to sit back and enjoy all of His creation. To rest, therefore, is to enjoy. To enjoy is to rest.

Think about a time you went to sleep only to wake up tired. I have. That's because I went to sleep but did not enjoy it. Consequently I was not rested. On the other hand you will find people who exercise or go for a run and find themselves refreshed and rested after a strenuous workout because they enjoyed every minute of it.

Now ask yourself: When did God create man? He didn't make him on the first day. Not on the second, the third, fourth, or even the fifth day. Instead God made man on the sixth day. I am convinced God did this so when man woke up on the seventh day, the first thing he would see was not God working but God resting or enjoying all that He had created. More significantly, God's desire was to enjoy creation with man. Henry and Richard Blackaby express our human tendency to be works oriented rather than to be relational. "We are so activity oriented that we assume we are saved for a task we are to perform rather than a relationship to enjoy."[2] The reason for our being was, and still is, all about relationship.

ENJOYING GOD

In his small book *The Dangerous Duty of Delight* John Piper explains how the authors of the old Westminster Catechism summarized the whole purpose of man's existence.

> "Man's chief end is to glorify God *and* enjoy Him for-ever."...Evidently the old pastors who wrote the catechism didn't think they were talking about two things. They said "chief end," not "chief ends." Glorifying God and enjoying Him were one end in their minds, not two....You do not have to choose between glorifying God and enjoying God. Indeed you dare not choose. If you forsake one, you lose the other.[3]

Piper is right. A relationship with God is exciting, exhilarating, and enjoyable. Like the way running creates a runner's high, a relationship with God produces spiritual endorphins that cause us to want to be around Him all the time, even in the midst of our pain.

Now consider what it's like running a marathon. The activity is full of unwarranted pain. Yet we find thousands of people take to it because they enjoy it. Doug Kurtis, who runs a dozen marathons a year, has a simple explanation for how he can withstand all the pain. "I don't train just to race," he says. "I run because I enjoy it....I enjoy being out there day after day."[4]

This is how Jesus's followers have been able to thrive in the midst of pain and suffering. They weren't following a strict code of conduct; they were enjoying a relationship with the One they loved.

ENJOYING SUFFERING

Following the Lord is about denying oneself and taking up one's cross. We need not invite suffering into our lives, for true discipleship will always involve some form of sacrifice and hardship. Jesus did say that living in this world would have its fair share of problems. Disciples are not exempted:

> Then he said to them all: "If anyone would come after me, he must deny himself and take up his cross daily and follow me."[5]

> In this world you will have trouble. But take heart! I have overcome the world.[6]

> But rejoice that you participate in the sufferings of Christ, so that you may be overjoyed when his glory is revealed.[7]

How can one be overjoyed as she participates in sufferings? Once again Piper explains it best.

> The chief end of man is to glorify God. And it is truer in suffering than anywhere else that God *is most glorified in us when we are most satisfied in Him....* And I pray that He would make it plain that the pursuit of joy in God, whatever the pain, is a powerful testimony to God's supreme and all-satisfying worth.[8]

Joy and pain don't sound right together, at least not to the "religious" and secular minds. The "religious" mind is usually more concerned with duty than it is with joy. The secular mind is the opposite. It abhors suffering because it cannot comprehend how that can be enjoyable. Unfortunately many Christians, even pastors and priests, have fallen into each of these mind-sets.

On the one hand there are those who insist on duty. Then there are those who believe that faith in Jesus equals a life of convenience and financial prosperity. Who in his right mind would welcome suffering unless it's a duty to be fulfilled, much less think of it as fulfilling and enjoyable? Yet the Bible insists:

> Consider it pure joy, my brothers, whenever you face trials of many kinds, because you know that the testing of your faith develops perseverance.[9]

> Not only so, but we also rejoice in our sufferings, because we know that suffering produces perseverance; perseverance, character; and character, hope.[10]

The only way to understand trials and suffering and how they relate to joy is in light of a relationship. As I write this book, I am enjoying a front-row seat to the day-by-day unfolding of two relationships, that of my twenty-seven-year-old son Joseph, who just got married, and that of my parents, who have been married for fifty-six years.

When Joseph was in courtship, his devotion to Carla was fascinating. He skipped meals, lost sleep, traveled great distances, and willingly sacrificed for Carla, the love of his life.

Joseph was never the type. But once smitten by the relationship, he changed, and those of us who have known him were amazed at his transformation. Joe became sweet and patient in the midst of inconvenience. He started to make sacrifices for the relationship. More importantly, he did it with great joy.

The other unfolding relationship is that of my parents. My father is eighty-one years old. A few years ago he underwent open-heart surgery. Recently he had another procedure to remove a cataract. Through my father's memory loss, arthritis pain, occasional drooling, and constant need to go to the bathroom, my seventy-nine-year-old mother continues to love him with a beautiful tenderness.

In celebration of my father's eightieth birthday she excitedly threw a party for him. Despite her lack of technological skill, she managed to create a PowerPoint presentation, complete with a video and photos of my father's life. Inviting relatives and friends who are still alive as well as members of the church, she honored him and brought him so much joy.

On the evening of the party my sprightly mother was beautifully dressed and coiffed sitting beside her husband, patiently wiping his mouth, attending to him, asking him for his choice of dessert, and personally serving him. Now after fifty-six years of loving my father and being loved in return, she shares in his suffering.

As the evening ended, I could see the gleam in her eyes and could not help but be reminded of the verse in Romans: "Now if we are children, then we are heirs—heirs of God and co-heirs with Christ, if indeed we share in his sufferings in order that we may also share in his glory."[11]

As C. S. Lewis has pointed out, the words of Scripture "were first preached, and long practised, in a world without chloroform."[12] The reality of suffering and pain in the first century was magnified in ways unimaginable to people of our time. Yet they shared in Christ's suffering. Then, just as now, joy in suffering makes sense only in light of a relationship. Only in that context can one understand how "the apostles left the Sanhedrin, rejoicing because they had been counted worthy of suffering disgrace for the Name."[13]

Enjoying One Another

From the very beginning God designed life not only so we could enjoy it with Him but also so we could enjoy it with one another. He said, "It is not good for the man to be alone. I will make a helper suitable for him."[14] He in turn not only created woman to be in fellowship with man, but He also designed our whole existence so we could be in relationship with others.

We were created to enjoy one another. The proliferation of social networks on the Internet is just further proof of the human desire to connect with others. God has placed in us a longing to be accepted and loved for who we are. We are hardwired for relationships.

From Adam and Eve have come twelve billion others, each one internally hardwired for relationships. Facebook works because it mirrors the LEGO Principle of connecting with one another. Churches and Christians who have learned to disciple through relationships will be the genuine phenomena over time.

But our wiring works only when we first enjoy a relationship with God. Unfortunately Adam and Eve were deceived into believing they could use the hardwiring solely for their relationship as a couple. That was a mistake. Our ability to relate with one another is only a product of our relationship with God.

My friend Wolfi Eckleben is the pastor of the Every Nation Church in London. He invited me to train his leaders on discipleship and wisely held the meeting at Edward's Pub in Hammersmith, a popular local hangout for twenty-somethings. He chose to host the training there to give it a certain feel and to send a message to his team: *Our role is to go and not wait for people to come to church.*

While having dinner after the sessions, one of the participants asked me a pointed question. To frame his question, he told a story about his friend: "Once to accommodate someone's request to know more about the gospel, my friend traveled forty-five minutes through the London subway and waited at the café only to receive a text message from the person saying he couldn't make it. The turn of events left him disappointed and frustrated, wondering if the time and effort he put into reaching out to others was worth it. Sitting alone at the café he thought to himself, 'What am I doing here? *Ugh*. What a waste of time.'"

Then came the question: "Who has time for this thing anyway?" Clearly this man and his friend were not enjoying discipleship.

I could relate well to this young man's story, as I have been in similar situations in the past. Who hasn't experienced frustration while sharing his faith? We all agree that as Christians there is a need to share one's faith with others, but there is so much fear and uncertainty in the act that we often shrink back from it. Most of the stress and anxiety I have felt in these situations came because I saw discipleship as a duty to perform.

When Christians approach discipleship from this perspective, it automatically changes the dynamic of reaching out. Christians become pushy in wanting to convert others. It's as if the security of their faith comes from getting others convinced that what they believe is true and right. This was never Jesus's posture.

When people do not respond to their advances, they get disappointed, frustrated, and eventually discouraged from building relationships with them. It is only when we realize that discipleship is first a relationship with God that we can enjoy the whole process of reaching out to others.

I am reminded of a time when I had set an appointment with a man who seemed to be genuinely interested to know more about the Lord.

When the appointed time came, he simply did not show up. After much preparation and expectation I felt frustrated as I waited and realized he was not coming.

Then a thought hit me: *Why should I fret when I have the whole time to be alone with God? Isn't that what this is about anyway?* Instead of moping and being discouraged, I decided this was a good moment to enjoy God. I read my Bible, prayed, and had a great time having coffee with the Lord and telling Him about my day.

If discipleship is a relationship, and my first and most vital relationship is with God, then who cares if no one shows up? It is only when we enjoy God and our relationship with Him that we will enjoy reaching out to others. And if there is anything true in life, it's that what we don't enjoy we will eventually stop doing.

I told the man at the pub: Imagine that your friend spent the forty-five-minute train ride praying and thanking God for all He had caused to work together for his good that day. It could have been a time to quiet his spirit while enjoying the ride and a moment to pray for the other passengers as well. By the time he arrived at the café, he would have been refreshed by the Holy Spirit.

And when he received the message that his friend was not coming, he could have used that time to read his Bible and spend an unhindered, undistracted, unrivaled evening with God. After all, discipleship is first and foremost a relationship with God.

Then when he'd had his fill of the Holy Spirit and his disappointment had subsided, he could have sent a text message back to his friend saying, "That's OK. I had a great time alone with God. It was awesome. Got to pray for you too. Let me know if I can be of service to you some other time. God bless."

When we are fulfilled by nothing but our relationship with God, we glorify Him in ways that impact those around us. Here again Piper is worth quoting, "God is most glorified in us when we are most satisfied in Him."[15]

This is the security we have when we understand that discipleship is relationship. When I am secure in God, nothing else really matters. I enjoy myself and other people, even those who reject the gospel. Their rejection does not affect His acceptance of me. God's grace and His love are more than sufficient.

Reflecting on the experience of this man's friend and similar situations I've been in, I discovered a tension. Every disciple should have an agenda that we do not hide. I am a Christian, and my full intent is to present the gospel to the people I meet with a desire to see them become disciples of Christ. This is not antithetical to enjoyment, love, or relationships. In fact, how can we truly claim to love people if we do not intend to lead them into a relationship with their Creator, who is the source of all life and happiness?

On the other hand, I have found that when I come to the meeting with "just an agenda," it usually does not work. When my intentions become my expectations and they are not tempered by a willingness to first build relationships, I often don't see positive results.

It's true that our relational encounters must be intentional and "missional." As we will see later, it is impossible to be truly relational without being deliberate and intentional, because relationships are always intentional. But we cannot become inflexible.

It's similar to when I go on a date with my wife. I used to attach too many plans to our evenings together—a specific movie time, a specific restaurant. And when my plans and expectations hit a snag—if she took her time getting dressed, we got caught in one of Manila's many traffic jams, or we couldn't get a table at a desired restaurant—I would be irritable and unlikeable.

An agenda is defined as "a list or outline of things to be considered or done."[16] While I have every intention of having a relationship with my wife, when I add a specific agenda, it changes the whole dynamic of our time together.

The same is true of the people we meet. If we come with just an agenda—expecting this person to make a confession of faith, come to church, or drop to her knees singing, "Glory, Hallelujah"—then we could be disappointed. No doubt we must be bold in proclaiming the gospel, but we must also use discernment in the way we present it and when to do so. So what's the right posture? Make it your mission and purpose to connect with people with the full intention of leading them into a relationship with God.

WHEN TWO WORLDS COLLIDE

I met Mark (not his real name) more than sixteen years ago. He was from Holland but had been residing in Manila for many years. I was officiating a wedding that Mark was covering as a photographer. At the time Mark was one of the most sought-after society photographers in the country. He lived a hedonistic lifestyle with his live-in partner.

To Mark, my world as a pastor and his world were nowhere near congruent. As Stetzer and Putnam put it, my world to him was "as intimidating, sobering, and irrelevant as it would be for many of us evangelicals to walk into a bar or club on Saturday morning at 1:00 a.m."[17] But there are many ways to engage people, even when we come from very different worlds.

The couple who got married are members of our church. They engaged Mark by contracting his services and simply being friendly to him. They also made sure he met their Christian friends who would not alienate him. I became one of Mark's acquaintances that day along with some others. We all engaged him during the wedding and in various settings afterward.

In time Mark came to church and became a part of a small group. Then I had to tell him the truth that apart from Jesus we are all in sin, but in Him there is forgiveness and new life. He eventually confessed his sins, prayed a sinner's prayer, and gave his life to the Lord. But my interaction with Mark underscores a very important point.

It's one thing to be relevant and relational; it's a totally different matter to succumb to relativism. Genuine Christianity makes an unpopular stand that draws the line between the truth and a lie while remaining relevant and relational. It does not blur the truth for the sake of relevance and relationship. After all, genuine relationships cannot be had without authentic truth.

Mark needed to know that Jesus was not simply a God he could capriciously keep in his pocket to assuage him of his guilt. He needed to know that Jesus is Lord and demands total devotion and lordship over his life.

Mark confessed his sins to God and prayed (which I believe was genuine) to receive the Lord, but his life did not transform instantly. In the meantime I kept the relationship with him, and his journey of faith began.

Mark's journey with God is no different from that of the prodigal son. Intellectually he knew he was a sinner and needed to repent, but the journey of his heart was not in step with what his mind had already believed. He was still too distracted enjoying his sins. But as in the case of the prodigal son, living without a relationship with God eventually becomes an empty existence. It's just a matter of time before a person's emptiness will cause him to recognize his need and come to his senses. It's always best to get to that place sooner than later. But sooner is not always the case.

Just as in Mark's case, there is a way of taking a stand for the truth while keeping a person attracted to the things of God. Much of it comes from being secure in our own relationship with God and how we value people.

Don't get me wrong. I'm not saying people will always like us or smile understandingly as we unpack the Scriptures. They may get defensive, become angry, or even walk out. But let that be over the message and not the way we delivered it.

I once asked Mark how he felt when I confronted him about the reality that his lifestyle was sinful and dishonoring to God. He said, "I knew you were telling me the truth, but I was not ready. But you were always nice to me."

It took many years for Mark to come to his point of need, but when he did, he knew exactly where to go. I kept the connection with Mark but helped him realize that following Christ will cost him.

Then one day Mark called me and asked if we could have lunch. After years of engaging him in a relationship, Mark's heart finally caught up with his head. He was broken, repentant, and ready to move forward with God. I am convinced Mark would not have made it to the place of true repentance had I not clarified the fact that he was living in sin and that it would cost him to follow Jesus.

The most significant part of this story is how Mark has engaged others for Jesus. There is no telling how many people he has brought into a relationship with the Lord. I can no longer count how many people Mark has introduced to me after church services, friends whom he has invited and testifies to about his changed life.

Mark reaches out one-on-one, whether he is in Amsterdam, London, New York, or Manila. He also engages friends in small groups and invites them to church. On occasion he will direct people to my blogs and podcasts in order to lead them to Christ. Heaven alone knows the amount of prayer and ministry he has sown into the hearts of people who are ensnared in a hedonistic culture.

Mark is an example of the thousands of disciples in our church who reach out to their friends and relatives. These disciples are responsible for the more than sixty thousand members who come every weekend to our ninety-one church services held in fifteen campuses overseen by teams of pastors.

JESUS'S MOST POPULAR PARABLE

There are relationship lessons we can learn from one of the Jesus's most popular parables, the prodigal son. When the younger son wanted to walk away from his relationship with his father, his dad willingly let him go.[18] He did not plead with him to stay or chase after him when he did leave. He simply made him know that he would accept him when he was ready to come home. So clear was this message that his son's first thought was to come home to his father once he came to his senses and realized the folly of his choices.[19] Home was his default option.

Two things generally cause people to come home to God, and both are evident in the story of the prodigal son. The first: *"He longed to fill his stomach with the pods that the pigs were eating, but no one gave him anything."*[20]

People run to God when they come to their point of need. Consider your own life. Many of us came to God because we were in need. Most of these needs fall into one of the following categories: relationships; health; financial and material lack; need for direction, purpose, or significance; or a spiritual need (i.e., salvation of family and friends). Clearly these are the things people value.

How do I know these categories? I've been reading them for years from church members who are asking for prayer. They may be written in different ways or with varying degrees of urgency, but they all fall into one of these groups.

Yet these needs are not the only reasons people finally come to God. There is a second impetus: *"When he came to his senses, he said, 'How many of my father's hired men have food to spare, and here I am starving to death!'"*[21]

I have found that while many people come to their point of need, they still have to come to their senses and realize that God is the answer to their need. Instead of trying to convert people, I patiently wait for them to come to their senses.

There are also those who know their answer is in surrendering to God but do not have a need at the moment. Likewise I wait patiently for the Holy Spirit to usher them to that place of realizing they are lost without Him.

When he reached the end of his rope, the prodigal son said, "I will set out and go back to my father and say to him: Father, I have sinned against heaven and against you."[22] When people find themselves at their point of need and come to their senses, they willingly change course, repent, and turn to God.

In the meantime my role is to stay connected to them. By our words and our actions we bear witness of Christ. We must continue building the relationship even if they don't believe yet.

There is a way of staying connected with people even when they are not ready to receive the Lord. Our role is not to convict or convert them. That's the work of the Holy Spirit.[23,24] Rather our role is to connect with people even when they are not ready to accept the Lord.

The parable of the prodigal son says, "While he was still a long way off, his father saw him and was filled with compassion for him; he ran to his son, threw his arms around him and kissed him."[25] While the Bible does not explicitly say it, the fact that the father saw his son "while he was still a long way off" indicates that he was constantly on the lookout for him.

We stay on the lookout for people through intercession. We follow up the work we've done in the spirit by staying connected through occasional calls, e-mails, text messages, or spending time with them.

God will give every human being an opportunity to recognize their need and come to their senses. How, when, and where this will happen we will never really know. What they need to be clear about is whom they can turn to when they are ready. This is the picture of God's patient love for us. As my friend Juray Mora would say, "If God can wait for people, so should we."

When the son returned home, his father was beside himself with joy. "The father said to his servants, 'Quick! Bring the best robe and put it on him. Put a ring on his finger and sandals on his feet. Bring the fattened calf and kill it. Let's have a feast and celebrate. For this son of mine was dead and is alive again; he was lost and is found.' So they began to celebrate."[26]

Notice how the father quickly restored his son into a relationship with him. He didn't say, "OK, it's great that you're here. Come back next week when I'm convinced about your repentance." Instead he immediately put a robe on him, a symbol of his righteousness,[27] a ring that restored his privileged position of authority,[28] and sandals that said you are not a slave but a son who has been made holy.[29]

The father wanted his son to enjoy all that he had. But he did not stop there. He threw a party and celebrated. Clearly our Father is a God who knows how to enjoy. What He really enjoys are restored relationships.

The Party Pooper

Typically the focus of the parable is on the prodigal son. We forget about the second half of the story: "The older brother became angry and refused to go in. So his father went out and pleaded with him."[30]

In contrast to the father, the older brother in the story is a sad picture of how Christians sometimes view life and ministry. They see discipleship not as a relationship to be enjoyed but as a duty to perform. Instead of celebrating the prodigal's return, the older brother was angry and refused to rejoice with his father and brother.

Yet even in his belligerence the father pleaded with his older son to come and celebrate with them. Here again Jesus is emphasizing that our Father is the God of reconciliation—the God of relationship.

> But he answered his father, "Look! All these years I've been slaving for you and never disobeyed your orders. Yet you never gave me even a young goat so I could celebrate with my friends."[31]

It's clear from this passage the older brother did not have an accurate view of how his relationship with his father should be. For starters, he did not even honor his dad by calling him *father*. And by his own confession he declared that he was just as much a slave as his brother—his kid brother in bondage to sin and him in his own self-righteousness and works. All this time he lived with his father and never enjoyed it.

When we don't enjoy our relationship with God, we end up counting and measuring what we have done. We feel entitled to wages rather than simply enjoying the relationship and everything God has to offer.

In his self-righteousness the older brother claimed he never disobeyed his father, which is something we all know cannot be true. Our own human efforts and religious works create a false sense of righteousness and pride.

How do we know the older brother was deluded? He said he was never given anything, yet the story tells us that the father divided the inheritance between his two sons. It was customary during those days for the older son to receive the larger share. Not only was he deluded about his self-righteousness, but also he didn't know how to celebrate and enjoy life even with his own friends.

Since he did not enjoy his relationship with his father, he could not celebrate his brother's return. Notice the older brother's words to his father: "When this son of yours who has squandered your property with prostitutes comes home, you kill the fattened calf for him!"[32] Not only would he not honor his dad by calling him *father*, but he also could not find it in himself to refer to his brother as *brother* either.

Instead of enjoying and celebrating with his father and brother, he accuses both of them—his father of being "too liberal" and his brother of being "undeserving." His was a world of laws and rules, religion and performance, and not of relationships that were meant to be enjoyed.

I appreciate what Dallas Willard has to say about enjoying God and one another: "The aim and substance of spiritual life is not fasting, prayer, hymn singing, frugal living, and so forth. Rather, it is the effective and full enjoyment of active love of God and humankind in all the daily rounds of normal existence where we are placed."[33]

LESSONS FROM THE PRODIGAL FATHER

To the very end the father wanted his older son to understand that his desire was for him to enjoy all that he had and to celebrate the relationships in his life.

> "My son," the father said, "you are always with me, and everything I have is yours. But we had to celebrate and be glad, because this brother of yours was dead and is alive again; he was lost and is found."[34]

The word *prodigal* means to be recklessly extravagant. The prodigal son's extravagant self-indulgence and the older son's self-righteous pride were no match for the "recklessly extravagant" love of their father.

This is a picture of our Father's desire to bring us back into a relationship with Him and His eagerness to celebrate our return at any expense. Discipleship is about relationship—a relationship that is to be celebrated and enjoyed. But while that's true, there's a whole lot more we need to understand about our discipleship relationships.

In the next section we will take a deeper look at what the Bible says about discipleship and why I believe it is all about relationship.

Not all LEGO pieces have the same ability to connect. Some have the capacity to connect with as many as twelve or more bricks while others are limited. There are pieces that can connect to only one other brick. The secret of LEGO is not that every brick connects with the same number of other pieces but that each piece has the capacity to connect.

The LEGO Principle that every piece has the capacity to connect was the revelation of a young Catholic monk back in the 1500s. He defined the doctrine of the "priesthood of every believer."[35] Luther believed that those who have been "born again" in Christ have the innate ability to connect directly to God. That connection is what gives all believers the ability to connect others to God.

One of the greatest setbacks of modern-day Christianity is that we have relegated ourselves out of the role of making disciples and depend on a handful of "full-time" or vocational ministers to do the job. This is probably the single biggest reason our discipleship efforts are not working as they should. Common sense alone should tell us that a lone minister building relationships with hundreds or thousands of people is both impractical and impossible. Every Christian must connect to God and to others.

SECTION II

RELATIONSHIP

4.

BUILDING BLOCKS

MY YOUNGEST SON, Joshua, and I like playing pranks on each other. One memorable evening after a grueling twenty hours of flights and stopovers from Europe, I arrived home exhausted. It was late, and I was looking forward to a good night's rest. The house was dark and silent. Not wanting to wake everyone, I quietly carried my bags up the stairway. Unbeknownst to me, my twelve-year-old son had crept out of his room to surprise me.

What made it so scary was I arrived past midnight. Joshua crouched behind a large wooden cabinet in the dimly lit hallway leading to my bedroom. There was nowhere to turn. Worst of all was that he was completely wrapped in a long dark brown Obi-Wan Kenobi hooded costume his older brother used in a high school student council publicity stunt.

As the child jumped right in front of me, you can imagine the heart attack he nearly caused me! Such are the games we play on each other. Truth be told, I love Joshua for it. But from that point on he and I have had a kind of "prank feud."

Sometime later while browsing in a novelty shop in Singapore, I found a rubber lizard that resembled the very same species we have in Manila. Without hesitation I bought the thing knowing how I would exact vengeance on Joshua.

A few days after I returned home, I positioned the creepy yellowish lizard inside Joshua's laptop and eagerly waited for him to come home from school. When Joshua arrived and entered his room, I stood by his doorway listening. I was hoping he would scream, but he didn't. He did get a momentary shock until he realized who was responsible when he heard me snickering behind him. Gauging from his stunned expression, I could tell I scored big that day.

I made sure I took the lizard back just in case he tried the same trick on me and put the thing on my dinner plate! Knowing Joshua, I figured it was just a matter of time before he'd think of a creative comeback. But what he did next was totally unexpected. While studying to prepare for a sermon, I opened my Strong's Concordance to check on a word, and there in between the pages was the lizard. No, I didn't scream, but I did let out an embarrassing yelp.

Just when I was about to pick up the lizard and put it back in my table drawer where I hid it, I noticed it was slightly larger than my rubber version. When I touched its stiff body and looked at its glazed eyes, I realized it wasn't a rubber lizard but a real, dead one! Much colder too! I had been keeping a rubber mouse, waiting for just the right time to prank Joshua with it, but after the dead lizard I decided to call it quits lest I end up with a genuine mouse inside my shoe. But who knows how long the truce will last. I still have the rubber mouse!

I love being a dad. After almost three decades of being a father, I've discovered that every child is unique, and there are distinct ways of connecting with each one. The key is to be a student of each child in order to learn how best to relate with him. Joshua, my youngest, is sociable and loves fun, engaging activities. David, our second, enjoys challenging pursuits, while Joseph, the eldest, has a deep interest in meaningful discussions.

As my friend Larry Osborne writes, all "relationships are completely different. No one-size-fits-all recipe can guarantee a great relationship."[1] But he is also quick to point out that while we are all different, we all have one Father, and He relates to us very differently. "If we really want to know him, really know him, it can be done through developing a personal relationship. And no two personal relationships will ever be exactly alike."[2]

Clearly there are different approaches when relating with people. However, I have found there are basic building blocks that are essential in any relationship, whether it's with our spouse, children, work associates, or even with God. These building blocks apply as well to discipleship.

If I say, "Discipleship is relationship," then it is vital that I clarify what

I mean by "relationship." This section of *The LEGO Principle* is dedicated to the four universal "building blocks" of effective relationships: trust, love, forgiveness, and communication. Only when we understand each of these four building blocks can we truly build lasting relationships with God and with others. Apart from just defining them, we will also look at how they apply to our discussion on discipleship.

We will see that life-giving relationships have been God's plan for us all along. But when sin entered the world, it severed that for everyone. We will examine the Genesis account of man's first sin and see how this spiraled out into fractured relationships for humanity. And we will see how Jesus's sacrifice restores our relationship with Him and with others.

THE AUTHOR OF RELATIONSHIPS

The account of God's creation in Genesis has always fascinated me. Imagine the entire universe coming into being as God spoke. First, the birth of light. Was it a gradual dawning or a sudden burst of brightness? Then came the colorful explosion of stars, planets, the heavens, oceans, seas, rivers, fish, mountains, volcanoes, seeds, plants and trees, birds, and all kinds of animals—all of them taking form at the mere sound of His word. Imagine the cacophony of brand-new sights, sounds, smells, and tastes!

If there should be a video in heaven of those first six days, it would surely put the most elaborate, computer-generated videos to shame. But more than all the rip-roaring, star-exploding, and rock-splitting action of those first days, what never ceases to astonish me is God's amazing and generous decision to create us so we could enjoy a relationship with Him.

Scholars tell us that one of the keys to understanding the Old Testament and what God wants us to know and understand in the text lies within the language of the narrative. When God created the universe and all matter, He identified Himself as the God of power. The language of the narrative depicted God as a single entity. All of a sudden when God created man, the language of Genesis shifted into the God of the Trinity, the God who had a relationship within Himself.

> Then God said, "*Let us make man in our image*, in our likeness, and let them *rule over* the fish of the sea and the birds of the air,

over the livestock, over all the earth, and over all the creatures that move along the ground."[3]

The unique thing about our God is He is one God in three persons. There is no God like Him. The significance of this truth is that He is capable of having a relationship within Himself. He did not create man because He needed him but simply because He *wanted* him. He loves man. It is also interesting to point out that when God made all the other creatures, they were made out of their own kind. But when He made mankind, He made them in His image, the image of the relational God.

This brings us to another significant aspect of this account of Creation. After God made mankind in His image and likeness, He also made them ruler over all of creation. Even the psalmist declares:

> What is man that you are mindful of him, the son of man that you care for him?...You made him ruler over the works of your hands; you put everything under his feet.[4]

What astounds me is how God took everything that was good and pleasing to Him and entrusted it to Adam. Why would He do that when in His sovereignty and foreknowledge He knew man would walk away from Him? I believe God did this because He was laying the foundation needed for all relationships: *trust.*

Trust is taking a risk. That's what God displayed when He entrusted His creation into Adam's hands despite His foreknowledge. In His infinite wisdom the Lord knew that for a relationship to work, there had to be a giving and keeping of trust.

THE VERY FIRST COMMAND

God's entrustment did not end with Him making man the steward of His creation. We see another display of trust in the first command He gave Adam.

> And the LORD God commanded the man, "You are free to eat from any tree in the garden; but you must not eat from the tree of the knowledge of good and evil, for when you eat of it you will surely die."[5]

It is liberating to know that God's very first command in the Bible did not begin with, "Don't do this..." Instead it says, "You are free," another statement of trust. Mankind was not just free but free to eat. Eating signifies enjoyment. Food is by far man's greatest addiction and one of his most pleasurable activities. Consider the sheer number of restaurants and products in supermarkets, the amount of time we spend cooking and eating, and the very fact that there is a Food Network, and you will see that eating is something we seriously enjoy.

From the very beginning our relationship with God made us free to enjoy what He has entrusted to us. God commanded Adam and Eve not only to eat but also to do so from any tree in the garden. This gracious gift of freedom was also about the foundation of all relationships: trust.

Trust is also the reason for the second part of the command and why Adam was told that he "must not eat from the tree of the knowledge of good and evil." Lasting freedom can only be had and maintained through trust. And for trust to be real it needs to be tested. Think of the pharmaceutical products and home appliances you have come to trust. You trust them because they have been tried and tested.

There was nothing mystically important about the fruit. The fruit restriction was a test to see whether Adam trusted God's word.

Without trust running both ways, there can be no relationship. You may live in the same house, ride in the same car, work in the same office, and even have the same surname, but without trust a relationship has no leg to stand on. It is just a matter of time before it suffers or ends.

Sadly, we often focus on the second part of the command. Like Adam and Eve we zero in on what we are deprived of instead of focusing on the generosity of the One who loves us and whose words we can and should trust.

Here is a way to look at it. Imagine a mall owner telling his twelve-year-old son: "The entire mall is yours to enjoy. Do as you please. Yep, everything. The video arcade, food court, movie theaters, Apple store, and, of course, all the LEGO pieces—everything! But *do not* eat of the pink cotton candy in the middle of the mall. If you do, you're definitely in trouble!" Guess what his son heads for? The pink cotton candy.

The tragedy of Adam and Eve's story is how they willingly sacrificed all their God-given privileges for the fleeting pleasure of one tree, just like the son who zeroed in on one stick of cotton candy rather than the freedom to enjoy the whole mall. The mistrust was never from God's side but from Adam's. Adam failed to realize that the foundation of all relationships is trust.

WHERE ARE YOU?

After Adam and Eve sinned, we find God walking coolly in search of them.[6] Obviously God knew what they had done and where they were. He is omnipotent and owns all the surveillance cameras in the mall. He had video footage of the kids' hands and mouth stained with pink cotton candy, so to speak. Yet He reacted to their sudden disappearance this way: "The LORD God called to the man, 'Where are you?'"[7]

If an omniscient, omnipresent God knew Adam's location and what he had done, why would He ask him this question? That's because His concern was not about Adam's physical whereabouts but the location of his heart. What He was asking him was, "Where are you now in our relationship? Where is your heart? Where is the trust I gave you?" Adam responded the way people typically do when trust is broken. He said, "I heard you in the garden, and I was afraid because I was naked; so I hid."[8]

Here we find the three results of breaking trust: fear ("I was afraid"), insecurity ("because I was naked"), and cover-up ("so I hid").

When God looked for Adam and Eve, it was not to scold or reprimand them but to restore the trust that had been lost. God knew that if the relationship was not restored Adam and Eve would spiral into a never-ending free fall into even more fear, more insecurity, and more lies. He knew that only in trusting Him would they be freed from this pattern of life. Only with Him would they have a good life, for He was their life!

In this account from Genesis we see how a disconnection from God will result in the tiring daily management of our fears, insecurities, and lies; a restless juggling act that makes for one exhausting life. This is our story without God. This is why trusting Him is so important.

To mitigate Adam and Eve's free fall into more fear, insecurity, guilt, and hiding, God engages Adam with two more questions. The first was:

"*Who* told you that you were naked?"[9]

This is yet another question about trust. God was asking Adam: "Who are you listening to? Are his words as trustworthy as Mine? Are you certain of his character? Do you trust him more than Me?" There was no response from Adam. So God asked him a second question:

> "Have you eaten from the tree that I commanded you not to eat from?"[10]

God asked this question to elicit the truth from Adam. God knew that trust is the foundation of relationships, and truth is the starting point of trust. Trust and truth are inextricably connected. Interestingly even their spelling is nearly the same. Unless Adam faced the truth, trust could not be restored.

Adam's response exposed the real condition of his heart. He did not want to deal with the whole truth. His trust in God was compromised. He had believed the devil's lie that he had the ability to be like God and that he would not surely die despite his disobedience.[11]

Rather than trusting God's love and desire to save him from certain death, Adam held his position of mistrust that God did not have the best of intentions for him and was withholding things from him. He had put his confidence in Satan's word over God's. He fell for the empty sizzle of the thought of being "god." Instead of answering the question and owning up to the truth, he blamed God for his own misdeed.

> The man said, "The woman *you put here* with me—she gave me some fruit from the tree, and I ate it."[12]

He blamed the woman and ultimately God for giving her to him. Another way of saying, "I don't trust You." The foolish thing about it all was God had made them in His image.[13] What the serpent deceptively offered was something God had already given. The only difference was that, as a good Father, God wanted Adam and Eve to learn what was good and evil not apart from Him but as they walked in a relationship with Him.

Sin deceives us into believing we can live a life without God. It is as C. S. Lewis once said, "We are all like flies on an elephant. He is infinitely greater than we are. To live in independence of Him is to live in delusion."[14] Adam had fallen for the delusion.

IT TAKES TWO TO TANGO

Unable to restore the relationship with Adam, God turns to Eve in the hopes that she would acknowledge her sin and restore the broken trust.

> Then the LORD God said to the woman, "What is this you have done?" The woman said, "The serpent deceived me, and I ate."[15]

Sadly she too would not face the truth of her own wrongdoing. The truth was, "When the woman saw that the fruit of the tree was good for food and pleasing to the eye, and also desirable for gaining wisdom, she took some and ate it."[16]

It wasn't just the devil's lure that made her turn away from God but her misplaced passions and desires that made her trust the words of her new friend, the serpent. There is a level of temptation where we can feign deception, but the Bible tells us that underneath all of it is a desire that drags us away into sin: "When tempted, no one should say, 'God is tempting me.' For God cannot be tempted by evil, nor does he tempt anyone; but each one is tempted when, by his *own evil desire*, he is dragged away and enticed."[17]

Eve hid behind the lie rather than face the truth about the state of her heart. This is how we often relate to God. The fact is, apart from His love and mercy we are inherently wicked, seriously lost, and spiritually dead. But God did not stop reaching out to them—such was His patience, kindness, faithfulness, and His love. God insisted on reaching out.

Realizing that Adam and Eve had been deceived by their own evil desires, God knew they needed a more compelling reason to turn back to Him: pain. Although they were deserving of death, God delayed judgment and instituted pain instead, because His desire was to restore the relationship.

Pain is the prelude to death. Pain was meant to give Adam and Eve a foretaste of death and what eternal separation from God felt like. In Genesis 3 we are introduced to the word *pain* for the first time in Scripture.

To the woman he said, "I will greatly increase your *pains* in childbearing; with *pain* you will give birth to children. Your desire will be for your husband, and he will rule over you."

To Adam he said, "Because you listened to your wife and ate from the tree about which I commanded you, 'You must not eat of it,' cursed is the ground because of you; through *painful* toil you will eat of it all the days of your life."[18]

Pain is the signal that tells us we are off course. For instance, when we have a headache, we know we need to quiet ourselves and rest. Pain lets us know our body is not functioning harmoniously. Or if our hand touches a hot stove, pain causes us to immediately withdraw it, thus preventing greater injury or even complete loss.

There is also emotional pain, which at times can be more distressing than physical pain. This is the kind of pain we experience when relationships are harmed or broken. Pain was God's way of forewarning Adam and Eve that they were headed in the wrong direction and if they continued, only death would be there to meet them. Here again is C. S. Lewis on pain:

> God whispers to us in our pleasures, speaks in our conscience, but shouts in our pain: it is His mega-phone to rouse a deaf world.[19]

Adam and Eve did not listen. Why should they? If they couldn't trust God for the good stuff, why would they trust Him for the bad? Adam and Eve had set themselves up for the free fall, and they would not be stopped.

Still God reached out with His precious love. Like a father who disciplines a child, He knew the pain He administered was still better than the greater pain they would experience without His love. Thus He issued a final warning:

> It will produce thorns and thistles for you, and you will eat the plants of the field. By the sweat of your brow you will eat your food until you return to the ground, since from it you were taken; for dust you are and to dust you will return.[20]

Let me paraphrase: "Adam, if you don't repent and turn from the direction you're headed in, life will be hard and will not be enjoyable. But worst of all, one day you will return to the dust you came from devoid of the breath of life I gave you."

Adam failed to realize an even more basic truth: God is still the supreme authority. Though God's nature, motive, and desires are rooted in love, He still is God, the sovereign authority over man. God's desire was for Adam and Eve to freely enjoy all of creation, but that freedom was not an offer; it was a privilege. To be more accurate, it was actually a command[21] that demanded their obedience.

VIOLATED RELATIONSHIPS AND PRIDE

This is the real problem of sin. It progressively hardens our hearts and separates us from God. The hardening of our hearts is not simply about our desire to do things that are sinful, but it is also about disregarding our relationship with God. As author Dudley Hall puts it, "The law defines sin in terms of violated rules, but grace defines sin in terms of violated relationships."[22]

I've always wondered why Adam and Eve did not just repent and get their relationship with God restored. Was it fear? Was it insecurity? Was it the lies and deception? I believe the answer is all of the above. At some point our fears, insecurities, and the lies we believe morph and harden into a heart of pride.

Fear and insecurity are actually the greatest motivators of pride. We are most prideful when we are most fearful and insecure, and we end up falling for the whole package of the devil's most devious tricks. We hide our fears and insecurities behind our lies. At some point we cross the line, preferring to be loved and accepted for who we're not than for who we are, not realizing that this isn't being loved or accepted at all.

Apart from God's grace, we deceive ourselves into thinking we can make life happen on our own without God. Instead of trust and love, Adam and Eve now bore the spirit of the serpent they had mistakenly believed, which was the spirit of pride.[23] Unbeknownst to them pride had ruled the day, and it continues to rule the hearts of men and women today. As Andrew Murray wrote, "Nothing [is] so insidious and hidden from our sight, nothing [is] so difficult and dangerous as pride."[24]

THE HEIGHT OF ARROGANCE

By now Adam's heart had hardened. After God's warning, instead of repenting and seeking forgiveness this was Adam's response: "Adam named his wife Eve, because she would become the mother of all the living."[25]

Commenting on this verse, John Calvin said, "Adam with thoughtlessness, who being himself immersed in death, yet gave his wife so proud a name."[26] Why did Calvin say this? Because it was Adam who had previously named his wife "woman."[27] Yet after being told they would surely die, he changes her name to Eve, which means "mother of all the living."

Adam's prideful declaration before God was, "Even if we are separated from You, we will still live." Adam not only mistakenly trusted the serpent's words over God's, but he also rejected God's offer of absolute love. When we are disconnected from God, life becomes an endless pursuit of what is true and right, and who we are.

Yet despite their guilt and Adam's arrogance, God further delayed judgment and instead extended His mercy toward them. By not responding with wrath and anger, God was attempting to stir them, yet again, to return to their relationship with Him. Notice what God did in the verse right after Adam changed Eve's name.

> The LORD God made garments of skin for Adam and his wife and clothed them.[28]

By now God had tried everything. Even pain and the threat of separation from Him could not get them to turn to the truth. The venom of the serpent's lie was too potent, and it had gone deep into their bloodstream. Now only blood itself could save them. Because of His desire to remain in relationship with Adam and Eve, God covered them with the skin of animals.[29,30] The new garments were the only way they could stand in God's presence without any shame.

Instead of killing them, which was the just punishment for their sin, God slew the animals that He entrusted to their care. The picture of the slain animals was (again) meant to jar them to the reality of their sin. Sin always kills. And death is always ugly. But it was also a picture of His mercy and forgiveness.

Imagine how Adam and Eve must have felt to wake up one morning and find the animals dead, blood and entrails spilled on the kitchen floor and the animals' ripped skins, warm with plasma, wrapped around their bodies. I wonder if these animals were lambs that Adam and Eve found to be the meekest and the cutest. The dead animals were to be a grim reminder of their fate—that without the forgiveness of sins, mankind's ultimate end is death. It was also a message that said, "Sin not only leads to our death, but it also hurts others." The bright red liquid was meant to communicate the seriousness of their predicament.

This was God's intent, His final attempt to stop their free fall into even more sin. Since they could not be stopped from their pattern of sin, He offered His forgiveness and spared them a sure death through the shedding of blood. This was the first prophetic picture of God's divine plan to send His Son, Jesus, the Lamb of God, to take away the sins of the world.

Instead of killing them, God showed His mercy and forgiveness in the form of atonement. Noah Webster's 1828 dictionary defines *atonement* as "satisfaction or reparation made by giving an equivalent for an injury, or by doing or suffering that which is received in satisfaction for an offense or injury."[31]

It is what we have often heard ministers term as a propitiation. Rooted in the word *propitious*, it means to be favorably disposed to someone. God, consistent with His character, holiness, and love for Adam and Eve, satisfied His own righteous law by imputing judgment on the animals instead of on them. As J. I. Packer points out, "The idea of propitiation—that is, of averting God's anger by an offering—runs right through the Bible."[32]

This is the reason Jesus, "the Lamb of God, who takes away the sin of the world,"[33] had to die on the cross: to cover our sins. As Tim Keller wrote, "There was a debt to be paid—God Himself paid it. There was a penalty to be born—God Himself bore it. Forgiveness is always a form of costly suffering."[34]

It is God's hope that through His act of mercy and forgiveness we will all realize there is really only one person we can completely trust. It was also His hope that Adam and Eve would receive His forgiveness and that they too would learn trust, love, and what it meant to forgive.

God's hope was that the garments of skin would make them realize that sin kills and only His mercy and forgiveness could keep them alive.

This was also the only way they could stay alive to still enjoy His favor and grace. For as Jesus said:

> He causes his sun to rise on the evil and the good, and sends rain on the righteous and the unrighteous.[35]

God is patient and kind. He is a loving and merciful God who forgives. But there was something just as urgent on God's heart. He knew that if the pattern of sin was not stopped, it was just a matter of time before Adam and Eve's descendants killed each other. God knew that His mercy would far outlast humanity's growing proclivity to sin. He knew that unless they learned His love and forgiveness, their sin was more dangerous than His judgment. Keep in mind that the very first recorded death in Scripture was not by God's doing but by a man named Cain, Adam and Eve's oldest son.

God knew that His kind of pain was nothing compared to the pain they were bound to inflict on each other. Nothing could be more painful than to watch your son die, even worse, to be murdered by his brother.

As we have seen earlier, God's desire was for man to know what was good and evil but not apart from a relationship with Him. This was the reason they could not be allowed to take from the tree of life and live forever. Man's capacity to know what is right and wrong does not automatically translate to an ability to live rightly, particularly in the area of relationships. Just "like Elizabeth Taylor, who has said that, with each of her eight marriages, she was convinced that somehow, someway, this marriage would work."[36]

God has designed it that only in a relationship with Him would they have the ability to live fully functional lives. It was God's hope that if He drove Adam and Eve from His presence, they would someday realize what they were missing.

> After he drove the man out, he placed on the east side of the Garden of Eden cherubim and a flaming sword flashing back and forth to guard the way to the tree of life.[37]

Now there was no way to enjoy the fullness of all of God. A flashing sword guarded the way back into the garden.

GOING FULL CIRCLE

At the center of our relationship with God is His eternal Word. Adam and Eve's relationship with God was founded on His word, and their trust in that word was the only thing that could keep their relationship intact. God's Word is the basis of all truth. Without it mankind is left to search for what is true. And since there is no source of absolute truth other than God, Adam and Eve were left to define what was right or wrong, good and evil. Now even their identities and in whose image they were made was questionable.

By Genesis 5 we see the fulfillment of God's word that Adam would "surely die." It says, "Altogether, Adam lived 930 years, and then he died."[38] God's Word came to pass. It may take as long as 930 years, but God's truth will always become a reality. His word is reliable; it is trustworthy.

When you think about it, Adam should have died instantly, but for the mercy of God. In His mercy God allowed several hundred years to pass to give Adam an opportunity to return to their relationship. In many ways that's what is happening with the passing of each year—God is giving us another opportunity to repent and fully trust Him with our lives.

The other important thing we see at the beginning of Genesis 5 is that man no longer bore the image of the God of relationships. The coming generations now bore the likeness and image of Adam.

> When Adam had lived 130 years, *he had a son in his own likeness, in his own image*; and he named him Seth. After Seth was born, Adam lived 800 years and had other sons and daughters.[39]

Unbeknownst to Adam and Eve, their internal hardwiring had been tainted by sin. While they still paid lip service to God, inside they were not the same. "Adam lay with his wife Eve, and she became pregnant and gave birth to Cain. She said, '*With the help of the* LORD I have brought forth a man.'"[40]

The trust of their hearts was no longer with Him. This is why just being religious is not enough. More than just believing a set of tenets, Christianity is about returning to a relationship with the Father—a relationship that was made possible only through a restoration of trust, and that is restored to us through Jesus.

For it was Jesus who took the punishment that was due mankind. He was the one who took the blows of the flashing sword that prevented us from partaking of the tree of life. His spilled blood gave us access back to the fullness of the garden.

FAITH: COMPLETE TRUST

The rest of Genesis 5 is a chronicle of the succession of the descendants of Adam, and there is a clear thread that runs through the genealogy:

> Altogether, Seth lived 912 years, and then he died.[41]

> Altogether, Enosh lived 905 years, and then he died.[42]

Then the story changes a bit when we come across one descendant who walked in a relationship with God.

> Altogether, Enoch lived 365 years. Enoch walked with God; then he was no more, because God took him away.[43]

There was no record of his death for he trusted in God's reliable truth. Another word for trust is faith. More accurately, faith means "complete trust." Hebrews 11 explains how Enoch escaped death.

> *By faith* Enoch was taken from this life, so that he did not experience death; he could not be found, because God had taken him away. For before he was taken, he was commended as one who pleased God.[44]

Our relationship with God begins with trust, the foundation that pleases Him. It is motivated by love, and restored and made new every day by His mercy and forgiveness. Trust, love, and forgiveness—these three are the primary building blocks of relationships.

In the next four chapters we will look at these three building blocks of relationship plus one more, communication, and how they each apply to discipleship.

At first glance the photograph looks like I am standing in New York City with the Manhattan skyline behind me. I wasn't. Actually I was in California at LEGOLAND. A closer second look at the picture shows that the buildings behind me were made of LEGO pieces. They were not quite the size of the buildings in New York; the tallest was probably just over twenty feet. But with my wife, Marie, behind the camera shooting the photo from the floor looking up, the buildings look massive.

Interestingly whether it's the Empire State Building, the Statue of Liberty, or a tiny phone booth on the streets of Manhattan, what allows LEGO Master Builders to create these masterpieces are the same plastic bricks designed more than fifty years ago to connect at the top and the bottom. In other words, some things just don't change.

Likewise, when we're making disciples (in any land), the key to having strong connections is through relationships built on trust, love, and forgiveness. Combined, these are the building blocks for relationships that last a lifetime. Some things will never change.

5.

TRUST

MY WIFE, MARIE, comes from a family of eight children. Whenever they get together for lunch or dinner, between her siblings and their children the gathering is more like an event than a family meal. In 2004 during one of these events our second son, David (who was twenty years old at the time), came to the dinner looking very scraggly. It was clear he hadn't shaved in some time. When one of his cousins asked him if he was trying to grow a beard, he replied, "Yup, I'll need it when I go to Afghanistan."

There was an uneasy quiet in the room as heads turned toward Marie and me. Words were not spoken, but the question hung in the air, "What possessed you to even allow your son to entertain this?" Later that evening one of Marie's siblings asked her privately about the trip and expressed genuine concern about the plan.

We understood their concerns. We had our own. The whole idea came about after David began planning a trip to Dubai using my expiring mileage points. When a pastor friend found out he was going to Dubai, he told him to include a stop in Kabul, Afghanistan, while he was in the region. My friend told him, "David, you'll never know what God can do through you unless you go." And that cinched it for David.

From that point on he tapped every resource he could to get a ticket to Kabul. In preparation for the trip he read about the nation. The more he read and saw pictures of Afghan children, the more he fell in love with the nation and its people. He was convinced he needed to go to serve.

Our church wanted to send much-needed volunteers to help the war-torn nation get back on its feet. There were opportunities to help: in Kabul University, with relief efforts, and with supply distribution. We had prayed and were convinced that it would be a good experience for David. That was then. Now that the trip was nearing, we were having some second thoughts.

THE TRUST FACTOR

We all trust at different levels and in different proportions. For instance, we may trust that God will meet all our material needs but are not quite as sure He will heal our diseases. Others trust that God can heal their sicknesses but are not sure He can fix their relational issues. Then there are those who can trust God for their lives but cannot trust Him for the lives of others. In short, trust is something that progressively grows. It increases as we mature in our relationship with God.

From the time David was born, our trust in God has been tested. When he was one month old, David needed immediate surgery when doctors found he had congenital hernia. With our hands clasped together, Marie and I prayed for a successful operation. Marie and I grew in our trust of God through David's healing and swift recovery.

In his first year of college David contracted the dreaded dengue fever, a disease that occurs in tropical Asia and in some South American countries. It is transmitted to humans by a mosquito bite and is also known as hemorrhagic fever because the virus can cause internal bleeding. A worrying symptom is when a victim's platelet count drops to significantly low levels. A small number of cases can lead to "dengue shock syndrome," a life-threatening situation that has a high mortality rate.

David had to spend a whole week in the hospital and miss classes for two months to recover. Unable to catch up with his lessons, he lost an entire semester of school. Again we saw how God healed and allowed him to continue with his education. Every time God came through, our trust grew. Now we needed to grow again in trust.

In the years my wife and I have been married, I have often relied on Marie's sensitivity. Though I am the head of our home, I lean on her for wisdom before making decisions. When David came to us with his desire to go to Kabul, Marie had questions, and I knew the only way to get the answers was to have a talk with David.

"You do realize that it is possible that you will not come home, right?" I asked. "You know it's possible that you could be killed." David looked at me quizzically as if to ask, "Where are you going with this?" Then he responded, "Wasn't it you who taught me to not be afraid of death? Didn't you teach us that in Jesus we have eternal life and that we have nothing to worry about?" For a brief minute I thought, "This is not what his mother would want to hear."

"Didn't you tell me that if I should be killed and people hid my body, God would hear my blood speak, even if they buried me under the ground like Abel? And that inevitably justice will be served just like what happened with him?" I thought to myself, "Did I really say that?"

I was stumped. He was right. David had grown in his trust of God while I had to move mine to the next level. His words were like a slap in my face that said, "You need to practice what you preach."

All Marie wanted to know was if David had prayed, sought counsel, and was sure God wanted him to go. David told her what he told me, and Marie had peace and trusted that God was in control. David went to Kabul that year and came home in one piece. Together we journeyed in trust and our faith grew. This is one of the building blocks of discipleship—growing in our trust of God and one another.

Several years ago a few of us at church developed an acrostic for the word "trust" to guide us in developing and teaching it. Obviously, it's not the real origin of the word, but we've found that it's helpful in breaking down this powerful truth into simpler concepts.

TRUST stands for truth, reliability, unity, standards, and time. Let's look at each of these elements of trust.

TRUTH

As we saw in the previous chapter, truth is the foundation of trust. Truth is becoming a rare commodity. We're so used to deceptions and half-truths that nobody gives them a second thought. Cynicism is at an all-time high around the world. We almost expect lies from government leaders, heads of corporations, media personalities, and, sadly, even religious figures. Videos and photos are edited to depict false realities. Image and appearance have surpassed substance and character.

Why do we trust God? Because "God is light; in him there is no darkness at all."[1] In another place the Bible says He is full of grace and truth.[2] Likewise as Christians we must be vessels of truth. The book *The*

Externally Focused Church points out well the need for trust: "'People have given up on the truth because they don't believe anyone can be trusted.' The world is full of people who have been hurt by those who were supposed to love them—people they should have been able to trust. Before churches will be heard, they must re-establish trust."[3]

Marie once taught me a great lesson in winning people's trust. Typically after I preach, she will immediately speak words of encouragement to me. When she wants to bring something up that is negative about my preaching, she will do it a day or two later when I'm more relaxed. On one occasion she pointed out something I said that was an exaggeration and that she felt I needed to correct. She was right—I had to face the truth.

The next Sunday I stood in front of the congregation and reminded everyone of what I had said and publicly apologized for my faux pas. At the end of the service several people came up to me and told me how much they appreciated my candor. One woman said, "Now I know I can trust you."

That day I learned that people are not looking for perfect people; they are looking for truthful ones. Everyone instinctively knows there is no such thing as a perfect person, so the more one tries to project that he is perfect, the less trust he generates. But the opposite also proves true; as counterintuitive as it may feel, coming clean, admitting our mistakes, and exposing our bad intentions is one of the quickest ways to begin building trust.

There is only one way we can consistently walk in the truth: by having a relationship with Jesus. After all He is "the way and *the truth* and the life."[4] This is why we can trust God and why we must develop a deep relationship with Him for He is "the Spirit of truth"[5] and "will guide you into all truth."[6]

The psalmist said, "Surely you desire truth in the inner parts."[7] Unlike Adam and Eve, who avoided the truth, as we draw near to God in relationship, we will be more truthful to God and to the world around us and build deeper relationships with others.

RELIABILITY

God is the ultimate picture of reliability. We can trust Him because His character and actions are consistent. The Book of Numbers expresses this truth best: "God is not a man, that he should lie, nor a son of man, that he should change his mind. Does he speak and then not act? Does he promise and not fulfill?"[8]

God is so reliable we can trust His promises:

For no word from God will ever be void of power.[9]

Not one of all the LORD's good promises to the house of Israel failed; every one was fulfilled.[10]

Let us hold unswervingly to the hope we profess, for he who promised is faithful.[11]

We know that the sun will be up every morning and the coming of the seasons will never cease[12] because God is reliable.

Before becoming a pastor, I was a businessman. In the world of business, transactions rise and fall on trust, particularly in the area of reliability. Whether it's with one's employees, coworkers, customers, suppliers, or bankers, our level of reliability will determine the level of trust people will afford us.

The key to being reliable lies in keeping things simple and following Jesus's advice: "Simply let your 'Yes' be 'Yes,' and your 'No,' 'No'; anything beyond this comes from the evil one."[13]

We become unreliable when we repeatedly give our word without following through. How many times have we made commitments such as, "Yeah, I'll call you tomorrow," only to shrug it off like it wasn't important? Or maybe we habitually set appointments only to cancel at the last minute or never show up at all. Sometimes as good Christians we promise to pray for someone without ever really doing it.

We also become unreliable when we take on more than we should. Our flippant attitude toward obligations sets us up for failure. Don't say yes when you mean no. Don't commit unnecessarily. Conversely don't say no to something when you have the ability to fulfill the need. Trust is not about little things or big things; it's about being reliable in our dealings. Can we really be reliable in *all* our dealings? Maybe not in all, but by simply being careful about what we commit to we can improve our level of reliability in most situations.

More significantly, we become reliable when we trust that Jesus is our ultimate source of functional dependability: "For no matter how many promises God has made, they are 'Yes' in Christ."[14]

Keep in mind what the Bible says: "The spiritual did not come first, but the natural, and after that the spiritual."[15] Our little acts of reliability, like LEGO bricks, build trust. Before people will believe our spiritual words, they will first look to see how reliable we are in our relationships.

UNITY

To have unity of the self means to be integrated. To be integrated means that each part combines to become a whole, an integer, a single digit, to be one. This is where the word *integrity* comes from. Trust cannot be had without integrity, or being unified.

God is unified. He doesn't change with the circumstances. Imagine the feat in writing the Bible over fifteen hundred years and remaining consistent with the message. As James puts it, He does not change like the shifting shadows.[16] God is one. He is unified.

It is here where the church has found itself in trouble. The reason the world is wary of Christians is because our beliefs, words, and actions are often not unified. This is what James called dead faith.[17] Faith that is not matched by a unified life is not real faith.

We cannot say we believe one thing yet behave in a manner that is contrary. While there is a similarity between reliability and integrity, we can be reliable in certain areas of our life and not in others. So while we may not be wholly unreliable, we also may not have every area of our lives integrated as one, which is what it means to have integrity.

To win the trust of the world, our lives must be unified and consistent. Would our coworkers be surprised by our piety in the church? Does our family, the people who know us best, respect us the least? Is our behavior guided by a trust in God and obedience to His commands, or do we change with the circumstance? Are our business practices congruent with our faith? Do we have integrity, a unified life? Can we be trusted?

As King David's life was coming to an end, he understood the kind of life that pleases God. He said, "I know, my God, that you test the heart and are pleased with integrity."[18] There is only one way to have a unified life of integrity, and that is to trust Jesus Christ as the sovereign authority of every sphere of our lives. He must be Lord and ruler over our personal affairs, family life, relationships, careers, and even our finances.

To quote a popular phrase, "If Christ is not Lord of all, He is not Lord at all." Only as we surrender every sphere of our lives to His authority do we become the disciples who have the integrity of a unified life.

When I was a single man and first starting out as a young entrepreneur, I had several business associates. One of them was a rather religious man who was several years older than me. He piously went to church every Sunday, had a good marriage and beautiful children, and was relatively successful in business. As a young single man I was raised in a "religious home," but one that could not be called Christian. As such I had my own share of misadventures.

Seeing my ungodly lifestyle, he would give me "older brother" discourses on what it meant to be a good husband (even though I was not yet married) and father. Somewhere in the discourse he would touch on matters of religion and church. I appreciated him for his concern for me. But his messages never really stuck.

His lectures did not have the credibility that comes with an integrated life. I would often find him reading "girlie" magazines and making imprudent advances toward other women. He would make inappropriate remarks that, though meant to be humorous, negated all his other good speeches. Worse were his unscrupulous business practices that were totally out of sync with his religious beliefs. You could say it just didn't compute.

In contrast when I met the man who discipled me, Steve Murrell, I saw someone whose lifestyle spoke volumes. He walked the talk. Whether it was in his marriage and children, his personal finances, his vocation as a pastor, or even just as a man, Steve embodied the integrated life.

Surely he was not perfect, but what you saw and what you heard were unified. From the very first day I met him to this day more than twenty-five years later, Steve has consistently demonstrated a life of integrity.

Without integrity our words fall to the ground and don't have authority. That's why my business friend's words did not have any impact on me.

The Bible says Jesus's words were different. They had authority, for He lived a life of integrity: "The people were amazed at his teaching, because he taught them as one who had authority, not as the teachers of the law."[19] Jesus was not merely a religious teacher; He is the holy God, who lived a unified life and whose words carry authority. Similarly our lives will win the favor of men based on how much integrity people see in us.

Truth. Reliability. Unity. Like the studs on LEGO bricks these are the connectors that allow us to build relationships with others. But those are not the only vital elements to understanding trust.

STANDARDS

Trust cannot be had without standards. A good way to illustrate this point is to look at a pig. A pig is truthful. It doesn't lie about being a pig. Talk to it, and it will answer, "Oink-oink." A pig is reliable. If you cut it open, it will produce ham, bacon, and pork chops every time. A pig is unified. It will be a pig yesterday, today, and forever. It doesn't change whether you bring it to church, to work, to the mall, or back to the farm.

But the very idea of putting our trust in a pig is laughable. Why? Because it's a pig! A pig has little to no standards and therefore is not the ideal symbol of trustworthiness. My example might sound silly, but I'm trying to make a point: truth, reliability, and being unified must be undergirded by standards. Without certain standards there can be no trust.

(Now to be fair, pigs are actually intelligent and sensitive animals. And they don't deserve the sweepingly bad stereotype that cartoons often attribute to them—of greed, gluttony, and filth. To be honest, some are more like Babe in the 1995 movie. But you understood the point.)

Much of life in our modern world works because we set standards. Think about the food we buy, the cars we drive, and the financial institutions we patronize. If they did not meet certain standards, we could not trust these products and services.

One of the businesses I used to run involved trade with Japan. Doing business with the Japanese meant meeting certain standards in order to complete transactions. The most basic were weights and measures. If a

Japanese importer ordered 500 tons of a certain commodity, he expected each ton to weigh 1,000 kilograms and nothing less. Likewise when we imported goods from them, we expected each container to have the exact number of pieces we ordered. And since our countries had different currency values, prices were quoted and payments were made in US dollars. These standards allowed us to do business with each other.

This illustrates is the importance of having appropriate standards. It sets the basic expectations on which people can establish relationships. Whether the relationship is between a husband and a wife, a child and parent, a friendship, or a business, standards are what form the common ground and the foundation for trust. Relationships established without standards to build on will not last.

How does God measure up in this regard? God is holy. He is trustworthy because His standards are infinitely higher than ours. His holiness is difficult for us to even understand. Bible teacher R. C. Sproul does an excellent job explaining the holiness of God.

> The primary meaning of *holy* is "separate." It comes from an ancient word that meant "to cut," or to "separate." To translate this basic meaning into contemporary language would be to use the phrase "a cut apart." ...He is higher than the world. He has absolute power over the world. The world has no power over Him. Transcendence describes God in His consuming majesty, His exalted loftiness. It points to the infinite distance that separates Him from every creature. He is an infinite cut above everything else.[20]

The first Anglican bishop of Liverpool, John Charles Ryle, defined holiness in these terms: "It is the habit of agreeing in God's judgment, hating what He hates, loving what He loves, and measuring everything in this world by the standard of His Word."[21] Standards are vital in our relationship with God for "without holiness no one will see the Lord."[22]

The apostle Peter wrote, "But just as he who called you is holy, so *be holy in all you do*; for it is written: 'Be holy, because I am holy.'"[23]

This is where trust comes full circle. The Bible tells us to "be holy in all" we do. It did not say *do* holy in all that we engage in but *be* holy. That's because holiness is not something we do but a standard we live by for all that we do.

Holiness is unattainable. It rests not on our abilities or self-righteous efforts but on the fact that God chose us to "be holy" even before creation out of His overflowing love for us. The apostle Paul wrote, "For *he chose us* in him before the creation of the world *to be holy* and blameless in his sight."[24]

The starting point to being holy is to put all our trust in the finished work of Jesus Christ on the cross. We are made holy not by what we do but by trusting in what Jesus did for us—to trust that it was God's choice and will to make us holy.

There is a principle that Bible scholars use in studying Scripture. It is called the "principle of first mention." What it means is that when a word is mentioned for the first time in Scripture, understanding that context is most likely an important part of understanding the definition and substance of the word. Can you guess where the word *holy* was first mentioned in the Bible? It was in reference to the seventh day in Genesis, the day God elected to rest and enjoy creation with man.

> And God blessed the seventh day and *made it holy*, because on it he rested from all the work of creating that he had done.[25]

Our holy God set apart this holy day so that in His holy presence man can enjoy His holiness. Think about it—holiness is not about trying harder but about resting and enjoying a relationship with God. The more we hang out with God, the more His standard of holiness becomes evident in us. It is not something we produce but something that is produced *in us* as we remain in Him.

Standards also matter in our relationship with the world. Sometimes Christians have the notion that in order to win people to Jesus, they must be popular. That is a mistake. Trust is what we're trying to develop.

Individuals and organizations who hold high standards are not necessarily popular. But when backed into a corner, people trust the ones who have held themselves a cut above the rest, whether doctors, accountants, bankers, teachers, or some other professional.

This is also true in leading people into a relationship with Christ. Jesus said, "In the same way, let your light shine before men, that they may see your good deeds and glorify your Father in heaven."[26] Some may not understand why we live differently, but when their world system comes crashing down and they see our good works, they will be drawn to God and glorify Him.

TIME

Time is the proving ground of truth and reliability. It is also time that produces proof of one's integrity. Adherence to standards is also time sensitive in the sense that we must demonstrate our consistent commitment to these standards over time. Time determines whether what we claim is real. In other words, trust is established over time. This, again, is why we trust the Lord: "Jesus Christ is the same yesterday and today and forever."[27]

But the more pressing issue is not just the passage of time but that truth, reliability, integrity, and standards are lived out consistently over time. Once again this is only possible as we continue to grow in our relationship with Jesus. He alone has passed the test of time consistently.

I am reminded of a story a church member recounted. One of his relatives came to him and said, "I have been watching you and your family for many years now. I was under the impression that your Christianity was a passing religious belief. But when I saw your marriage, children, and the way you have lived your life, I realized that you have something I don't. You have faith." It was just a matter of time before his relative became a Christian along with his family.

What are we doing when we're making disciples in small groups? Simply put, we're creating an atmosphere and culture of trust. We're teaching people to learn to grow in their trust of God so they can enjoy His holy presence and the holy life He has ordained for us. We are also teaching them to learn to grow in trusting one another in order to win the world's trust.

Each LEGO brick comes with studs that give it the ability to connect. Every stud has the LEGO trademark engraved on it, a symbol of trust. In the past others have tried to copy LEGO bricks but have been unsuccessful. Their studs did not connect as well.

Like trusted LEGO bricks, we connect best when we are the real thing. When we trust God and are trustworthy, connecting to Him and to one another is simpler and easier.

A quote from Korean War veteran and former Franciscan priest Brennan Manning is the best way to end this chapter and usher in the next: "Only love empowers the leap in trust, the courage to risk everything on Jesus, the readiness to move into the darkness guided only by a pillar of fire. Trust clings to the belief that whatever happens in our lives is designed to teach us holiness."[28]

6.

LOVE

EARLY IN OUR marriage Marie and I realized that going on a date on Valentine's Day was not the easiest thing to do. Traffic is usually a nightmare, restaurants are crowded, and service is predictably slow. Not to mention that the prices of flowers and chocolates skyrocket. It can make you wish you owned stock in Flowers.com and See's Candy. So when our sons were very young, instead of going out, we celebrated February 14 as a "family love day" rather than a romantic evening for Mom and Dad.

One Valentine's Day the boys woke up to find Marie had prepared a special breakfast of heart-shaped pancakes served on a table set with a red tablecloth and matching paper napkins. In each of their school bags she put a note from Mom telling them how special they were. For recess that day they had heart-shaped Dunkin' Donuts stashed inside their lunchboxes.

By midday Marie had called to remind me that tonight was Valentine's dinner, her way of alerting me to be home early and ready to engage the children. Undoubtedly she is a much better parent than I am.

Over dinner the conversation naturally turned to the topic of "love." Like posing a question to a small group to warm things up, I asked my sons, "Do you know that when you get married (and have a wife like Mom), half of what you own will go to your wife?" I decided to put this in terms I knew three boys aged ten and below would understand. "That means half of all your G. I. Joes and half of all your LEGO pieces will go to her. Of course, you'll also get to share half of her Barbies."

My hope was that they would realize that getting into a relationship was a serious thing, so that when they reached their teenage years, they wouldn't jump into one flippantly. All that explanation of love, caring, and sharing of toys brought funny and touching remarks from my seven-, nine-, and ten-year-old sons.

Joseph, our wise eldest son, solemnly declared, "Then I will make sure that I marry someone I really love." Honestly the maturity of his answer surprised me. I'm certain he inherited that trait from my wife's side of the family. True enough, Joseph waited and did find someone he really loved and is now married to her.

David, our enterprising middle son, seemed horrified by the idea. His eyes grew wide and he blurted out: "What? Give up half of all my G. I. Joes? Then I won't get married!" David eventually graduated with a degree in economics, became a savvy and hardworking businessman, and, yes, is still unmarried! This one looks like he came from my side of the family. I don't think he was very excited about receiving Barbies either.

Joshua, our youngest, sat quietly. I could imagine his seven-year-old brain processing. "When you marry, you share half of everything?" I nodded. Then without a moment's hesitation his eyes lit up and his face beamed and he replied, "Then I will marry a billionaire." From which side of the family this one comes still baffles us to this day. My point is this: if three young boys from the same family had three different takes on love, how many more takes are there in an entire world?

AN OVERUSED WORD

No word is more used, defined, written and sung about than *love*. No wonder it is so misunderstood—too many definitions always produce confusion. But the love we're talking about in the context of discipleship cannot be just any kind of love; it has to be God's kind of love.

Since we are created in the image of God, we are able to love at a certain level. Undoubtedly we love our spouses, children, parents, friends, those we like, and those who do us a measure of good, as well as those we choose to love for any number of other reasons. Our love quotients vary from person to person depending on our background, exposure, tastes, inclinations, and even our resources. Often our ability to love is dependent on how healthy or unhealthy our relational experiences were growing up.

Some are inclined to love more than others. But regardless, comparing one's love with another's is not the way to go, because our love levels don't measure up to God's standard. They have been tainted and corrupted after what the Bible describes as "the fall." God's kind of love is pure and unconditional. It is a love that we have no clue even exists unless the Holy Spirit reveals it to us.

Author Oswald Chambers expressed it this way: "No man on earth has this passionate love to the Lord Jesus unless the Holy Spirit has imparted it to him.... The only Lover of the Lord Jesus is the Holy Ghost, and He sheds abroad the very love of God in our hearts."[1]

God's kind of love is beyond human comprehension because it is not a feeling, not an emotion, not a decision. Love is a person, for "God is love."[2] As significant and profound as this statement is, many people still misinterpret it. Filipino theologian William Girao sheds light on this common misunderstanding.

> "God is love," the apostle John tells us. Everything that God is, love is. The converse, however, is not true. It is inaccurate to say that everything that love is, God is. Love by whose definition? Love by whose experience? Love as modeled by whom? This, in fact, is the idolatry of our generation. We have deified "love." But love by the definition or experience or standard of anyone except by the perfection of God is imperfect love, not genuine love. And anything imperfect is not of God.[3]

Adam and Eve made a poor choice to walk away from God, for when they did, they walked away from love. Yet God insisted that our relationship with Him be one of love, a kind of love that cannot simply be defined as benevolence, obedience, self-sacrifice, grace, or mercy, but all of the above and a whole lot more.

As I pointed out earlier, the unique thing about our God is that He is a triune being. It is from this truth that we get the word *Trinity*. Theologian Wayne Grudem writes, "God is three persons. Each person is fully God. There is only one God."[4] An attempt to explain the Trinity in this brief chapter would be futile. Great men have written exhaustively on the subject. Grudem's *Systematic Theology* is one excellent and accessible example.

The fact is, the more you study the Trinity, the less you understand it.

But then again, what kind of God can be fully explained and understood? God is infinitely an infinitude—He is limitless!

The implication of the Trinity is what is important to our current discussion. Unlike other so-called gods, our God in three persons personifies a God of relationships, a God of love, a God who is capable of love on His own. After all, it is impossible to love someone when there's no one to love. But since God is a Trinity, He is able to experience love within Himself.

It also explains the fact that God did not need man to have someone to love. He was whole in His relationship to Himself. He created mankind not out of a need; His motive for creating mankind was nothing but pure love.

THE FIRST BLESSING

After God created mankind, He blessed them. Do you know the words of God's first-ever blessing to mankind?

> God *blessed them* and said to them, "*Be fruitful* and increase in number."[5]

I used to gloss over this verse because I mistakenly thought that being fruitful and increasing in number meant one and the same thing. I reasoned that being "fruitful" is just another word for "increase" and that the repetition was God's way of emphasizing His desire to see us populate the earth. I was wrong.

The Bible uses two different words to express being fruitful and increasing in number because they represented two distinct parts of the blessing. Being fruitful means to have so much life that it naturally manifests in offspring or fruit. It has been said that fruit is the result of an abundance of life. Fruitfulness also means to flourish, to thrive, to grow in healthy ways, to be luxuriant. As we become fruitful, we will naturally multiply and increase in number.

Adam and Eve were created with a seed in their hearts that was designed to bear fruit—to flourish, grow, and then increase in number. I am convinced that the seed is God's love—it was His desire that His love grow and mature into a fruit that would then multiply. But the seed could grow only if God was in the center of their hearts. Much like the way a seed dies without the nourishment of the sun, God's love grows only when God who is love is in it.

In Galatians 5 the apostle Paul writes: "But the *fruit* of the Spirit *is* love, joy, peace, patience, kindness, goodness, faithfulness, gentleness and self-control. Against such things there is no law."[6]

This verse has been the subject of much discussion, primarily because it uses the singular noun "fruit" and the verb "is" and yet the rest of the verse lists a variety of possible fruit. Even more intriguing is a verse that comes before it: "The *acts* of the sinful nature *are* obvious: sexual immorality impurity and debauchery."[7]

This verse uses the plural noun "acts" and the verb "are" then itemizes each of the acts of the flesh. Why would the apostle Paul use a singular noun and verb for the "fruit of the Spirit" and use a plural noun and verb for the "acts of the sinful nature"?

Bible translators were exacting when they translated Paul's epistle. They took note of the emphasis he made on the many acts of the sinful nature by using the plural verb "are" for the acts of the flesh. But why was the singular verb "is" used for the fruit of the Spirit?

Martin Luther gave this explanation: "It would have been enough to mention only the single fruit of love, for love embraces all the fruits of the Spirit."[8] Clearly Paul believed, as Luther expressed, that there was but one fruit of the Spirit—love.

Paul was also careful to use the word "acts" for the flesh and "fruit" for the Spirit. Acts of sin are things we do out of our own volition and decision. Love is a fruit that requires a relationship with God, for He alone has the ability to grow love in our lives.

But how does one make sense of the verse if it says "the *fruit* of the Spirit *is*," using a singular noun and verb, yet follows with a list of qualities that includes joy, peace, patience, kindness, goodness, faithfulness, gentleness, and self-control? These characteristics are not in addition to the fruit of love, but rather the resultant attributes of a fully mature fruit of love, much like the color, texture, flavor, nutrients, aroma, juice, substance, and seeds of a single ripened fruit.

As we grow in our relationship with God, the fruit of the Spirit (which is love) grows too. The result is we become more joyful, peaceful, patient, kind, good, faithful, gentle, and self-controlled.

In the past when I read these verses I thought I was pretty joyful, peaceful, patient, etc. As I grew older, I realized that developing each of these qualities of love is a lifetime endeavor that can be achieved only as I remain in a relationship with God.

Take patience, for example. I may have grown patient in loving my wife with regard to the amount of time she takes to get dressed. But I have yet to become more patient when I'm busy doing something important (like surfing the Internet) and she wants to talk with me. And while I may have grown in patience in relation to my wife, I may still have much more growing to do when it comes to my dealings with other people.

Growing in patience alone will require a lifetime. How much more will growing in joy, peace, and the rest of these qualities of love? Only as we remain in a relationship with God will the fullness of the color, texture, and flavor of our love become fully ripened and mature.

Luther's idea makes more sense when we cross reference Galatians 5:22–23 with 1 Corinthians 13:4–7, which is in the famous chapter of the Bible celebrating the beauty of real love. What we find is a happy marriage between the two:

GALATIANS 5:22–23	1 CORINTHIANS 13:4–7
Love	Love
Joy	Rejoices in the truth
Peace	Not self-seeking, not easily angered, keeps no record of wrongs
Patience	Patient
Kindness	Kind
Goodness	Does not delight in evil
Faithfulness	Always protects, always trusts, always hopes, always perseveres
Gentleness	Not rude
Self-control	Does not envy, does not boast, is not proud

The above chart further supports Luther's idea that love is not only *a* fruit but is *the* fruit of the Spirit. More significantly, the lists describe the character qualities of God. It seems that if we grow in this one fruit, we would deal with many of the issues that create problems in life and relationships. Is it any wonder that Jesus said all the commandments boil down to loving God? As we love God, we become like Him and are able to give His love to one another.

DISCIPLESHIP AND THE FRUIT

What finally convinced me that love is the first blessing of fruitfulness is the fact that Jesus taught this. In John 15 Jesus speaks of how the fruit of love grows in our lives through our relationship with Him.

> *Remain* in me, and I will *remain* in you. No branch can bear *fruit* by itself; it must *remain* in the vine. Neither can you bear *fruit* unless you *remain* in me. I am the vine; you are the branches. If a man *remains* in me and I in him, he will bear much *fruit*; apart from me you can do nothing.[9]

According to Jesus, one must remain in the vine to bear fruit, and He is that vine. On our own we are incapable of producing anything. By remaining in a relationship with Him we will bear much fruit.

Jesus then said, "This is to my Father's glory, that you *bear much fruit*, showing yourselves to be *my disciples*."[10] When we bear much fruit, we prove ourselves to be Jesus's disciples. The question is, what did Jesus want His disciples to remain in? Jesus tells us in the very next verse: "As the Father has loved me, so have I loved you. Now *remain in my love*."[11]

The love of the Father, as it is manifested in Jesus, is the very life that is produced in us—the fruit that shows everyone that we are His disciples. In another place Jesus said, "By this all men will know that you are my disciples, if you love one another."[12]

Love is the motive of all discipleship relationships. It is actually the motivation that drives all successful relationships. If we are really serious about being disciples and making disciples, we must grow in the fruit of love—not just any kind of love but God's holy love.

Love at Another Level

God—the pure, perfect, all-powerful, ever-living, ruler of the universe—came to earth and inconvenienced Himself to become one of us. His reason: to show us His love.

God not only revealed His love by coming to earth; the greatest demonstration of the power and quality of His love was at the cross. "But *God demonstrates* his own love for us in this: While we were still sinners, Christ died for us."[13] It is one thing to love someone when we have reason to do so—our spouse, children, friends, and those we like. God loved us "while we were still sinners." In short, He loved us even though we were His enemies and rebelling against Him. He demonstrated His love by sending His Son to die on the cross for us despite our fallen state.

What exactly do we glean from the picture of the cross? God is holy. He is perfect and without fault. He cannot tolerate sin in any form since this is totally against His character. His standard of holiness is beyond our own ability to reach. So pure and holy is He that we cannot even begin to approach His presence.

The severity of this holiness has made Him unapproachable by those who have even a hint of sin. This is the holy God who flooded the earth to purify it from sin.[14] This is the holiness that frightened the Israelite nation in the desert.[15] This is the holiness that had Isaiah trembling in the temple[16] and the same God who will judge all men in the last days.[17]

Because God is holy, He cannot tolerate sin; therefore our sin separates us from Him. The wages of sin is death only because we are separated from God. In His righteousness and holiness God has ordained punishment for the sins of man, and as sinners we all deserve to die. But for some reason God delayed our punishment and diverted it to His Son instead so that we may live!

God's irresistible, severe, and all-encompassing holiness was tempered only by His equally irresistible, powerful, and unconditional *love*! His love is one of a kind—it is holy. Bible teacher Kevin J. Conner explains this holy love God demonstrated:

> God in His love desired to save the sinner. God in His holiness must execute His wrath and judgment upon sin. How could this be done? God could not manifest love at the expense of His

holiness, and again, God could not save the sinner without judgment upon the sin. What has to be done? The judgment for sin was death (Romans 6:23). What was the answer? It is found in the atoning work of Jesus Christ. Through the cross God deals in absolute holiness with sin and in perfect love with the sinner.[18]

This is the demonstration we see at the cross: holiness and love in perfect harmony. Pastor Tim Keller put it this way: "On the cross neither justice nor mercy loses out—both are fulfilled at once. Jesus's death was necessary if God was going to take justice seriously and still love us."[19] This kind of holy love is the very one that Lennon and McCartney may have intuitively referred to when they wrote about money not being able to buy them love.

THE ULTIMATE MNEMONIC DEVICE

The cross is Christianity's ultimate mnemonic device. Sadly, while symbols of the cross abound, a series of wrong ideas have been contrived about what the cross truly means. These ideas have somehow emptied the cross of its power[20] because it has become a mere religious icon no longer symbolizing what it was meant to convey: God's holy and undying love for mankind. We are sinners who deserve death several times over, but we are alive today only because of His great love.

People ask, "If God is all about love, why do we have to keep talking about Jesus and the cross? Why can't we just trust that He loves us?" It is because only in understanding the cross—and the justice and holiness it represents—will we understand God's love. As Tim Keller explains, "The answer is that if you take away the Cross you don't have a God of love."[21]

God's love is the eternal fruit that He wants to grow inside of us. The way He ordained to get that seed planted inside us was to send "the Seed" of His love, His Son, Jesus Christ. The apostle Paul wrote, "The Scripture does not say 'and to seeds,' meaning many people, but 'and to your seed,' meaning one person, who is Christ."[22] He is the one who must become greater as we must become less.[23] Christ is the one who chose to be last so we could become first. It is the fruit of this seed that God wants to multiply and increase in number. This He does as we remain in a relationship with Him.

DISCIPLESHIP AND LOVE

As we discussed, God's first command to Adam and Eve gave them freedom to enjoy His creation. This was rooted in His desire to develop a relationship with man built on love. God knew that for love to be love, it could not be imposed, demanded, contrived, or manipulated. For love to be genuine, it has to be freely given and freely received or freely rejected. That's why He gave Adam, Eve, and the rest of us the freedom to walk away from His offer of love.

When we abide in a relationship with God in Christ, we grow in the fruit of His love. As we thrive in that relationship, the fruit of love in us grows. When we freely administer the same love to others, they too will begin to grow in His love. This is how the fruit is multiplied on the earth.

In His wisdom the Holy Spirit used the picture of a fruit for us to understand what love is and how it grows. Yet while fruit grow and mature, they also rot. Like everything else in God's creation, there is a period of growth and maturity. As we grow and mature, we cannot just rely on our past actions and gestures of kindness. We need to keep growing fresh and new fruit that can be given to others.

On the one hand we must grow and mature in patience, kindness, and all the other qualities of love. On the other hand we must always remain "amateur." *Amateur* comes from the Latin word *amator*, or lover. An amateur does things out of love, not for any other recompense. When we become experts at love, we've begun to miss the point.

To be an amateur means to constantly acknowledge that we will never fully comprehend God's love; we never become "professionals" at love. But as amateurs we willingly and excitedly look forward to fresh and new seasons of fruitfulness, a never-ending journey of discovering of God's love in fresh new ways.

And this is true of human relationships, isn't it? With our spouses we begin to lose our joy in the relationship the moment we become "professional" at loving each other, when we do it in exchange for something else. "I'll scratch your back if you'll scratch mine." This is no longer love but a negotiation, a contract.

The world is already full of relationships built on contracts and obligations. What's increasingly becoming rare are unconditional relationships built on love. When we receive that love from God, we can show it to others. It is a love that keeps giving, a love that can accept people regardless of their background, a love that goes beyond loving those close to us to loving even our enemies. Just the way Jesus showed us.

PERFECT LOVE FOR AN IMPERFECT WORLD

Here's a final story bring home my point. On a recent trip to China to equip local church leaders, I was picked up at the airport by two young men who were amazing disciple makers. Making disciples in the big cities of China is not an easy thing. The growing material prosperity and years of telling people there is no God can be challenging. Yet these men are successful at making disciples. One in particular was prolific. He was responsible for growing a steady stream of young disciples in his bustling city. He successfully did it by building relationships with them. Whether it was hang time at karaoke bars or playing video games, he did it all just to reach them.

Over dinner he told of a situation he had with a lady who was part of his group of disciples. He framed his story by saying that after a year of being part of the church and being relationally connected to other women in discipleship, she had fallen into immorality. The day before she moved to another city for a work assignment, she had gone on a one-night stand that totally caught them by surprise. When she returned, she did not come back into fellowship but pursued a life away from the Lord and His people.

His voice was both sad and had a hint of frustration. He asked, "How do I get her to come back to God?"

I said, "By loving her with the perfect love of Christ."

To this he said, "I have tried, but she has not responded."

I told him, "That's because your love, like mine, is imperfect. For starters, love is patient, and you are getting impatient that she is not responding. Imagine if God became impatient of our sins; the whole world would be wiped out in a day. Fortunately His love is perfect."

"So what do I do?" he asked.

I said, "Preach the gospel of Jesus Christ to yourself every day."

"What do you mean?" he asked.

I told him that I have made it a practice to preach the gospel to myself every day. I remind myself that I'm a sinner and that apart from God's love and mercy I am living a hopeless, helpless life that is in terminal decline. I am in deep debt, and there is no way out apart from God's never-ending love to bail me out. By acknowledging this truth, I am able to tap into the fullness of His love for me, a source of confidence I have learned to depend on every day.

I recounted to the young men the story of a close friend who incurred a sizeable financial debt. I knew there was no way for him to pay. I entertained the thought of helping him pay the debt to alleviate his family from the pressure. But the reality was that I did not have the capacity to pay for it. And when I seriously thought about it, I most probably wouldn't have paid for his debt even if I did have the money. That's because my love is imperfect. Perfect love necessitates both desire and ability. Only God has both.

What I did instead was to give my friend a substantial amount of money and told him that was all I could afford and that he did not need to pay it back. Even that limited act brought him to a place of seeing God's perfect love moving through an imperfect man like me.

The real key is to always stay connected to the vine, to experience God's perfect love daily. The more we get of His love, the more we are able to give of it. This is the fruit the whole world is craving, the very one I am able to give away as I experience it for myself each and every day.

Two Movies

One of my wife's favorite romantic movies is *The Notebook*. The movie is based on the novel by best-selling author Nicholas Sparks. My all-time favorite romantic movie is *The Man From Snowy River*, based on the poem of Australian bush poet Banjo Paterson. While *The Notebook* is what I'd call a "chick-flick" and *The Man From Snowy River* is an Australian adventure classic, both have a similar love story theme. A girl from the rich side of town meets a working-class boy and falls in love. Both relationships face challenging odds as parents' and society's tastes and dictates come to bear on their relationship. Against all odds we who are watching can see how right it all is. We quietly cheer and pray that somehow, someway they will make it together.

What is it about this theme that resonates so well with us that we keep coming back for more? From the dawn of storytelling, whether it's Belle and the Beast, Elizabeth Bennet and Mr. Darcy, or movies such as *Sabrina, Titanic, Notting Hill* to the more recent love story of Edward and Bella, each of these stories portrays something extreme, something that could not possibly be, and yet something that we all bear witness to. We all wish someone would love us in this extreme way, someone who would willingly throw away the comforts, security, fame, and fortune and risk it all because we are worth it.

This is what the world is looking for—passionate, radical, extreme love. So why does it resonate so well with us? Because we have been wired on the inside for such a kind of love. But the truth is only One Person can love us in this way. This is the love of God that we find in Jesus Christ. When we, His disciples, learn to walk in His love, we will have the ability to extend the same love to others. This is the only real hope of reaching a lost world!

"Two eight-stud LEGO bricks can be combined in twenty-four ways. Three eight-stud bricks can be combined in 1,060 ways. Six eight-stud bricks can be combined in 102,981,500 ways. With eight bricks the possibilities are virtually endless."[24]

Just like LEGO bricks, using love to connect with people has endless possibilities. There are a variety of ways by which love can be expressed, and each expression opens the way to even more possible connections and relationships.

Robert Coleman, a seminary professor who writes frequently about discipleship and evangelism, calls love the "credentials for ministry."[25] He writes:

"Love—Calvary love—was the standard. Just as they had seen for three years, the disciples were to give themselves in selfless devotion to those whom the Father loved and for whom their Master died (John 17:23). Such a demonstration of love through them was to be the way that the world would know that the Gospel was true. How else would the multitudes ever be convinced? Love is the only way to win the free response of men, and this is possible only by the presence of Christ within the heart."[26]

7.

FORGIVENESS

J OEY, YOU CAN'T do that!" I can still hear my wife's protests. "Trust me, I know what I'm doing; my father did the same thing to me," I replied. (I should have realized that's why I turned out the way I did.) My two sons Joseph and David were misbehaving in the car. I had warned them to stop their wrestling and scuffling several times, but being playful little boys, they paid no attention.

As an inexperienced young father, I found that sometimes unorthodox parenting techniques would turn up. At times the results were good, and at other times they bombed (seriously). This was one of those times when I messed up big-time. In order to teach the boys a lesson, I parked the car, took my sons out, plopped them on the sidewalk, and told them I was leaving them there until they behaved. To Marie's horror, I then drove away.

I actually advanced but a few feet from them, but how could two little boys ages five and four know the difference? We were vacationing and were in unfamiliar terrain, an open field that to them did not look anything like our hometown. A few seconds later I backed up the car and picked them both up. They quietly sat in the backseat like two little mice in their corner. "There. See, I fixed it." Or so I thought.

I glanced in the rearview mirror and saw David quietly fiddling with his fingers. I then looked at Joseph, my five-year-old. What I saw was a picture I would never forget for the rest of my life. The expression on his face was a mixture of confusion and fear no child should ever have to experience. I felt for him, but I fought the emotion rising up in my chest and told myself, "He is my eldest, and he will need this lesson to be a man." I consoled myself saying, "Hey, look at me. I made it, and I'm strong." Actually, I was wrong. Very wrong.

That would soon become abundantly clear, but in the meantime I had to fix the more pressing problem of Marie. She was furious with me for leaving her babies on the sidewalk that way. I knew it was the doghouse for me that night.

Eleven years later as I sat at home praying, the Lord reminded me of that day. I vividly remembered Joe's face in the backseat of the car. I wept from the bottom of my heart, realizing how wrong I was. After wiping away my tears, I asked Joe if I could speak with him. Though we were very good friends and he has been a blessing of a son, I knew I had to make things right.

I brought him to my little office at home, and we sat facing each other. I asked him hesitantly if he remembered that day. He looked at me with his warm eyes and quietly replied, "Yes, like it happened yesterday." I asked him how he felt that day as a five-year-old. He said, "I was so afraid that a lion would come and eat us, and I couldn't protect my brother."

Joseph had a vivid imagination—so vivid that in just seconds he had conjured the beast and was already worried about how to fend it off and protect his little brother. What was a matter of seconds to me must have seemed like forever to him. A thrown pebble has little effect on an adult but could cause serious injury to a child. I was ready to bawl for inflicting this unwarranted pain on my son.

I knelt before him with tears now gushing and said, "Joe, I am so sorry. I was wrong. I did not know how to be a good father then." I could sense he knew how affected I was because I was shaking as I wept. Joe took my head, trying to console me, and said, "Pop, Pop, I forgive you. I know you didn't mean it. I forgive you." He held my face with his hands and kept saying, "I love you, Pop." I responded, "I love you too, Joe."

When I share this story, people often remark about how great a moment that must have been for Joe, and they are right. To forgive others sets you free. As we have heard it said before, "Not forgiving is like drinking poison and expecting the other person to die." Joe had to let go of whatever offense and bitterness he may have had because of the incident. It set him free.

But equally important was the fact that I was forgiven that day. My sin was removed and wiped away like it never happened. It would be an experience I would cherish for the rest of my life. I get the same feeling each day I am reminded of how God constantly forgives me. To experience forgiveness is a powerful thing. To be forgiven is both humbling and liberating because true forgiveness erases our past infractions and wipes our slate clean. Today Joseph and I can look back at the incident with no bitter feelings. Instead we look back and see how God brought us to a place of victory instead of animosity. My son and I were strengthened in our relationship.

The incident also taught me a vital lesson about relationships. When fathers and leaders model a willingness to repent of their mistakes, they end up teaching their children and the people they lead how to forgive. Unknowingly I began a culture in my family that day, one in which people forgive one another easily.

BE PERFECT

Jesus said, "Be perfect, therefore, as your heavenly Father is perfect."[1] Our life experiences should be enough to convince us that of all Jesus's commands, this one is not going to happen, because we all have different ideas about what it means to be perfect. But the context of this verse can only be fully understood when read together with the verses that preceded it.

> But I tell you: Love your enemies and pray for those who persecute you, that you may be sons of your Father in heaven. He causes his sun to rise on the evil and the good, and sends rain on the righteous and the unrighteous. If you love those who love you, what reward will you get?[2]

It was after Jesus spoke these words that He said, "Be perfect, therefore, as your heavenly Father is perfect." Jesus was not talking about perfection the way we understand it. To us, perfection is about our personal performance, our so-called "good deeds" and accomplishments. Often perfection means success in the way our world defines it. We also think it means never making a mistake.

To Jesus, perfection is all about the way we keep our relationships—particularly how we treat our enemies and those who hate us. It is easy to love those who like you but not those who are trying to oppress you.

Unlike loving those we like, loving our enemies and those who persecute us starts with forgiveness. To be more precise, it starts with forgiving as God forgives us.

Forgiveness is God's provision for restoring relationships. It is what can restore a broken trust. It is what revives love that has faltered. It is the reset button of relationships. It is what "reboots" relationships that have gone sour. It refreshes every day of our lives. That's why the Bible says, "The steadfast love of the LORD never ceases; his mercies [forgiveness] never come to an end; they are new every morning; great is your faithfulness."[3]

The arrival of every refreshed morning is a reminder of His love, mercy, and forgiveness. Just as St. Augustine has pointed out, "viewing the Creator through the works of his hands, raise up our minds to the contemplation of the Trinity, of which creation bears the mark in a certain and due proportion."[4]

This was his manner of saying, one of the ways to see God as He relates to us is by observing creation as it is revealed in every new day. The psalmist affirms Augustine's point: "The heavens declare the glory of God; the skies proclaim the work of his hands. Day after day they pour forth speech; night after night they display knowledge."[5]

Each new day is a declaration of God's mercy and forgiveness. One reason we don't understand God is that it is hard for us to contemplate His forgiveness. How can someone who has absolute power, complete perfection, and impeccable excellence love so much and be so forgiving? Thank God, we're not God, for we can be an unforgiving people.

I'm sure you've heard stories about people who have done so much good but then have a moment of weakness and fail. From that point on they are remembered for their mistakes, while their good work is, for the most part, relegated to the dustbins of history. Ours is an unforgiving world of performance. As I have grown older, I have come to embrace the wise words of John Wesley, "The longer I live, the larger allowances I make for human infirmities."[6]

Wesley's point comes from realizing that because of man's proclivity to sin the only remedy for frayed relationships is forgiveness. No doubt people will suffer the consequences of their actions; that's justice:

"Righteousness and justice are the foundation of your throne; love and faithfulness go before you."[7]

In the midst of God's righteousness and justice, God sends out His love and faithfulness first. In another place the Bible says, "Mercy triumphs over judgment!"[8] God designed it so that His forgiveness is made available fresh every day. That's because without forgiveness all relationships, including our relationship with God, will end. This is the perfection Jesus was telling His disciples we should learn and put our faith in.

ANIMALS VS. FRUITS

The best way to understand forgiveness is to know how sin works and how it affects our relationship with God. As Pope John Paul II explains, "Man, who was created for freedom, bears within himself the wound of original sin, which constantly draws him towards evil and puts him in need of redemption."[9]

As we have seen with Adam and Eve, sin disconnects us from God and changes the way we view life. But that's just the beginning of the story. Like love and grace, sin also grows, multiplies, and gives birth to death. The Bible says, "Then, after desire has conceived, it gives birth to sin; and sin, when it is full-grown, gives birth to death."[10]

What seemed to be an insignificant matter of Adam and Eve disobeying God and partaking of a forbidden fruit had more disastrous repercussions as it progressed to the next generation. Here is the continuation of the story:

> In the course of time Cain brought some of the fruits of the soil as an offering to the LORD. But Abel brought fat portions from some of the firstborn of his flock. The LORD looked with favor on Abel and his offering, but on Cain and his offering he did not look with favor. So Cain was very angry, and his face was downcast."[11]

Cain and Abel both made offerings to the Lord. Abel brought animals; Cain brought fruits. In God's righteous sovereignty He rejected Cain's offering and favorably received Abel's. If you're like me, your humanistic tendency probably has you wondering what kind of God would show partiality in such a small matter as an offering. What's the big difference between fruit and livestock anyway?

Abel did not offer flocks to the Lord simply because he was a shepherd. Nothing he did in that passage was by chance. His offering came from a deeper revelation, one that was founded on faith. The writer of Hebrews said:

> By faith Abel offered God a better sacrifice than Cain did. By faith he was commended as a righteous man, when God spoke well of his offerings. And by faith he still speaks, even though he is dead.[12]

By observing his parents' garments of skin, Abel knew by faith what God desired even before God asked for it. Surely it may have influenced his decision to be a sheepherder. He may very well have been earth's first evangelist. That is why "by faith he still speaks, even though he is dead."[13]

Cain's offering was rejected for a reason: it was not done in faith but by his own works or abilities. After Adam and Eve sinned, God had cursed the ground and declared that by the sweat of their brow they would produce fruit from the ground. What Cain was offering was a product of his own works, and it was simply unacceptable.

Herein lies the fundamental truth about forgiveness. We are not forgiven because of anything we do. We cannot earn forgiveness. Rather, it is extended to us by the sheer kindness, favor, and love of God—it is only because of His grace.

MASTERING THE BEAST

"Then the LORD said to Cain, 'Why are you angry? Why is your face downcast? If you do what is right, will you not be accepted?'"[14] Once again, as in the case with Cain's parents, God extends His mercy and tries to elicit the truth from Cain. And Cain, like his parents, refused to face the truth and insisted on being the judge of what was good and evil, right and wrong.

God in His mercy was making Cain realize that deciding what was right and wrong was not up to him. Cain needed to understand that he was not God and never would be. No amount of insistence on his part could turn what was wrong to right. Like his parents, Cain needed to understand that God was the authority over his life. And only through God's forgiveness could his life be made right.

Yet like his parents, Cain avoided responding truthfully to God. Within one generation Adam and Eve's sinful attitude had morphed into belligerence. Still God entreated and encouraged Cain to make the right choice and master sin.

> But if you do not do what is right, sin is crouching at your door; it desires to have you, but you must master it.[15]

In this verse we find that sin is described as a living creature, a predator that crouches slyly waiting for those who will open the door of their heart. God was warning Cain that if he did not master sin, it would end up mastering him.

The key was to not let this vile creature in. It was one thing to be tempted and fight the creature from without. It was a totally different thing to open the door and be controlled by it from within. God was warning Cain that if he allowed the creature in his life, he would not only be in an internal prison, but he would also be enslaved by a cruel master—sin. This was the fight the apostle Paul described in Romans:

> For what I do is not the good I want to do; no, the evil I do not want to do—this I keep on doing. Now if I do what I do not want to do, it is no longer I who do it, but it is sin living in me that does it.[16]

God had warned Cain, "Don't let the creature in." Yet again like his parents, he did not listen. We know the rest of the story. Pride prevailed. Cain opened his heart to sin and killed his brother.

INSECURE FALSE GODS

Today much of the world recognizes the wisdom of the sixth commandment: "You shall not murder."[17] But unforgiveness follows us still. While most of us don't literally kill people, we erase them from our roster of our relationships rather than enjoy them for who they are in God. Often we tolerate their existence rather than explore the possibility of having a relationship with them. Even here we have decided what is good and evil about people. We have become judges and attempted to take on a role that belongs to God.

People don't make good gods. We were never created to be one. We become bullies, pharaohs, emperors, tyrants, dictators, and manipulators. The only thing that differs is the size of our domain. It could be a playground, a kingdom, an empire, a company, an office, a home, a marriage, a friendship, a small group, even a church. Without the one true God at the center of our hearts, we end up with a society of false gods who cannot distinguish good from evil.

When you think about it, we aren't too different from Cain. With Cain it was about having a better offering. With us it could be: Who has the most accomplishments? Who has the better marriage, nicer kids, bigger house, cooler toys, better career, higher jump, longer stride, faster time, or most friends? Who is the fittest, firmest, prettiest, smartest, richest, and so on?

Without the righteousness of God, life becomes a daily struggle of "one-upmanship." It becomes the tiring pursuit of what is true and right. Even more daunting is the constant grappling to discover who we are and what we're worth. As Tim Keller put it, "Identity apart from God is inherently unstable. Without God, our sense of worth may seem solid on the surface, but it never is—it can desert you in a moment."[18]

We are left to delude ourselves by comparing our actions, accomplishments, and way of life with others'. If we can somehow convince ourselves that we are not too bad, we'll be fine. This is the only way we can again feel good about ourselves. Sadly once our guilt and insecurity are assuaged, it is just a matter of time before we again need to convince ourselves that we are not too bad, and the cycle of "one-upmanship" continues.

Unfortunately there is nothing out there that can cover our guilty consciences. As my friend Paul Barker is known to say, "Guilt is one of the most painful, if not the most painful, of emotions." He supports this idea by pointing to the many people who engage in stringent religious practices that result in excruciating pain, such as those who beat themselves to identify with suffering of Jesus. Some spouses even accept violent treatment because they feel guilty about their failed marriage. Lewis Smedes can only agree; he writes: "The family name of pain is 'guilt.'"[19]

This kind of self-harm may temporarily cover one's guilt and pain, but the relief will be short-lived. Only God's forgiveness can totally cover our guilt, pain, and shame. As the Scriptures declare, "Blessed are they whose transgressions are forgiven, whose sins are covered."[20]

Drawing from Cain's story, it seems the ugly roots to outdo one another started not with the secular aspirations of mankind but with a religious offering. Among the religious we find this struggle alive and well. Who has the correct theology? Who has the deeper truth? Who has the better practices? Who is the better preacher? Who has the largest flock? Who has served more? Who reads his Bible more? Who is meekest and humblest? Who has the latest, greatest revelation? Are your sins venial or mortal? Who is "perfect"?

But none of these are ever enough to completely cover the fear, insecurity, guilt, and pain we bear without God. That's why Cain was offended that his offering was not accepted. He could not bear the thought that he was wrong and his brother was right. Guilty, angry, depressed, and despondent, Cain found himself in the prison of his own sins, and without forgiveness he had nowhere to turn.

I've had some people ask me...

How Forgiveness Works

Some say, "If God has truly forgiven me, why then do I still need to repent? If I'm free of my debt and am no longer guilty, why do I still need to repent?" These questions reveal a misunderstanding of grace and forgiveness. This thinking reduces forgiveness to an absolving of consequences but not a restoration of a relationship. On the one hand, forgiveness is a legal tender, but it is also a means of reconciling broken ties.

Forgiveness means God has unlocked the prison doors of sin that enslave us. Repentance makes us acknowledge our sin, thus allowing us to realize we are in prison but can now walk out. Those who like Adam, Eve, and Cain refuse to repent and acknowledge their sins end up staying in prison even when the door has been unlocked. They remain slaves even though their sins have been covered and paid for.

The prodigal son in Luke was forgiven long before he came home. But his forgiveness would not have had any effect if he had not returned home to receive it. That's why we are called by God to repent. It's like He's saying, "Turn around and come home. You have been forgiven."

God doesn't demand that we repent because He wants to rub our infractions and guilt in our faces. It's His way of getting us out of prison and back to enjoying a relationship with Him. Forgiveness is something God has freely extended to mankind, but it takes effect only when we acknowledge our need to be forgiven and receive that gift freely. As I have written earlier, how can we be forgiven if we have done nothing wrong? In the words of the prophet Isaiah, "Let the wicked forsake his way and the evil man his thoughts. Let him turn to the LORD, and he will have mercy on him, and to our God, for he will freely pardon."[21]

THE WORST PLIGHT OF ALL

Meanwhile back to Cain. After he killed his brother, Cain was confronted by God.

> Then the LORD said to Cain, "Where is your brother Abel?" "I don't know," he replied. "Am I my brother's keeper?" The LORD said, "What have you done? Listen! Your brother's blood cries out to me from the ground."[22]

In this passage we see God reaching out in hope that Cain will face the truth. He asked him where his brother was. And true to his parents' form, Cain responds with an ambiguous excuse designed to avoid facing the truth. God then exposes his lie and consequently his heart. Still Cain would not own up to his sin. The verse below shows that he was more concerned about his ability to manage the punishment meted out to him than with restoring his relationship with God.

> Cain said to the LORD, "My *punishment* is more than I can bear."[23]

Like Adam, Eve and Cain, we are often more concerned with the penalty of our sins rather than the true condition of our hearts. Our concern is not about being restored in a relationship with God; rather we are concerned about how to assuage our guilty consciences. Francis Chan writes about our human tendency to manage our punishment.

> This is why I have so many people ask me questions like, Can I divorce my wife and still go to heaven? Do I have to be baptized

to be saved? Am I a Christian even if I am having sex with my girlfriend? If I commit suicide, can I still go to heaven? I am ashamed to talk about Christ, is He really going to deny knowing me? To me, these questions are tragic because they reveal much about the state of our hearts.[24]

Gripped by pride, Cain chose to remain in the prison of his sin. Without God's forgiveness, Cain would suffer the worst plight of all: restlessness.

Now you are under a curse and driven from the ground, which opened its mouth to receive your brother's blood from your hand. When you work the ground, it will no longer yield its crops for you. You will be a *restless wanderer* on the earth.[25]

Banished from God's presence because of sin, Cain would suffer the consequence of his unrepentant heart. He had cursed himself. Now no longer was he just managing his fears, insecurities, lies, and pain. The cycle would result in a life of restlessness. Whereas God's original plan was for mankind to rest and enjoy Him, now Cain would be deprived of rest and enjoyment.

God's hope was that the stark contrast between His original plan of rest and enjoyment in His presence would drive Cain to the place of humility and repentance. It didn't. Cain had imbibed the intoxicating prideful spirit of the serpent. He refused to admit his sin and need for God, and he foolishly chose a life of restlessness over a relationship with God.

Without the daily acknowledgement of God's forgiveness and our constant awareness that we have been freed from the prison sin once trapped us in, our lives become a never-ending rigmarole of restlessness. Only in Christ are our sins forgiven. And only in Jesus can we be restored back into fellowship with the Father to again enjoy His rest. That's why He invites us to come to Him.

Come to me, all you who are weary and burdened, and *I will give you rest*. Take my yoke upon you and learn from me, for I am gentle and humble in heart, *and you will find rest for your souls*.[26]

Let me put this all together. Sin separates us from God. Without God we end up trying to be gods left to decide for ourselves what is good and evil. The result is a world full of insecure, confused, deluded, foolish, hopeless, angry, depressed, and restless pseudo-gods who live the daily grind of trying to cover ourselves up. It's no wonder the world does not work. Without God it never will.

Sin wreaks havoc on our relationship with God, our relationships with others, and even within our very own soul. Only the forgiveness of God cancels all the penalties of our errant ways and cleans the slates. It begins the process of restoration that will eventually undo even the worst works of sin in our lives. That's what makes forgiveness so important.

People often ask, "If God is about love and forgiveness, why then does He send people to hell? Why did He even create hell?" Like Cain, we are guilty of focusing on the management of our punishment instead of asking the right question, "Why would a holy God of love allow a reprobate sinner like me to even have the opportunity to enjoy heaven with a perfect God like Him?"

An even more important question is, "Why would the Father send His Son to die so my sins could be covered and I could enjoy the privilege of being His child?" The only real answer is because of His love and forgiveness that exceed our human comprehension unless the Holy Spirit reveals it to us.

DISCIPLESHIP AND FORGIVENESS

Often making disciples is about programs to teach people how to behave as followers of Christ. It focuses on increased commitment and stricter discipline—all designed to produce a lifestyle of sacrifice, holiness, humility, and worship; the lifestyle of a disciple. Later we will see the value and importance of discipline when we understand it from the viewpoint of a relationship.

But if we are not careful, this approach could devolve into the same mind-set Cain had and turn into just another human effort to cover up our own nakedness. This is even more insidious because it has the appearance of piety and devotion, but it is so close to sin. The line can be easy to cross, just as Cain so easily went from offering a sacrifice to committing murder when it didn't give him the desired results.

It's not that these disciple-making practices are wrong. The issue is that unless we first receive the forgiveness of God in Christ, our lives are spent in a constant and futile pursuit of covering, performance, and "being perfect." In teaching others to become followers of Jesus, the critical factor is to help them understand the depth of our sinful nature and the immensity of God's mercy and forgiveness toward us.

The apostle Paul wrote, "Therefore, I urge you, brothers, *in view of God's mercy*, to offer your bodies as living sacrifices, holy and pleasing to God—this is your spiritual act of worship."[27] Paul was saying that when we have a correct view of God's mercy (His forgiveness), we will offer our bodies as living sacrifices, and we will aspire to be holy to please God, which are our spiritual acts of worship.

When we have a clear understanding of our true nature as self-righteous, destined-for-hell sinners who are lost in the quagmire of our own evil pride yet have been forgiven by a holy, loving, and perfect God, our attitude toward life changes. Our attitude becomes one that says, "It is only reasonable that I offer my body as a living sacrifice." We willingly set ourselves apart as those called to a life of holiness to be instruments in the hand of our God.

When we understand God's forgiveness, we walk humbly before Him. We understand that humility is not about lowering ourselves from a higher position, because that only produces even more pride and self-righteousness. Rather, we realize that humility is acknowledging how low our true position is and that it is only through God's mercy and forgiveness—His grace—that we are saved, healed, and restored into a relationship with Him. With this understanding there is no abuse of God's grace.

It is with this revelation that we can fearlessly enter into relationships with one another and the world. We know that we will let each other down, but we also know that we can forgive and be forgiven. We cannot let anything cause us to quit on one another.

One of the biggest stumbling blocks the world has when considering the church is the amount of infighting and sniping that goes on among supposed brothers and sisters. Whether it's hurtful words exchanged on a national media level or silent (or not-so-silent) feuds in home Bible studies, division among believers is antithetical to Jesus's commands.

Very often, when people attempt to bring about reconciliation, we get too enmeshed in the details of the faults. Even if a resolution can be agreed upon, it's often entered into begrudgingly, opening the door for hostilities to resume.

Instead what's needed is a fresh start, a wiping away of everything that has gone before, a willingness to trust and reach out again. That's forgiveness. That's what God did for us. And that's what we will do for one another as we continue to thank Him for forgiving us.

ALL FOR ONE, ONE FOR ALL

Trust, love, and forgiveness—these are the first three building blocks of relationships. If we are to be technical about it, all three fold into one in love, for we are told that love "always trusts"[28] and it "keeps no record of wrongs."[29] Even more significant is the fact that each of these building blocks is found in the blood of Christ, which is the ultimate expression of God's love for us.

- We put our trust (or faith) on nothing but Christ's blood: "God presented Christ as a sacrifice of atonement, through the shedding of his blood—to be received by faith."[30]

- God's love has freed us through His blood: "To him who *loves* us and has freed us from our sins by his *blood*."[31]

- We have been forgiven through His blood: "This is my *blood* of the covenant, which is poured out for many for the *forgiveness* of sins."[32]

This is yet another picture of how God's kingdom works, not in linear, sequential, compartmental dichotomies but in lives brought together by a loving, faithful, and merciful God. Discipleship is relationship, first with God then with one another. It is about growing in trust (faith), love, and forgiveness. And as the verse says, "All things work together for good to them that love God."[33]

The LEGO brick was invented in 1957 and was patented in 1958 for its stud and tube coupling system. This is what's magical about the LEGO brick's ability to connect. When LEGO bricks are removed from one another, they can easily be rejoined because the removal hasn't damaged their ability to reconnect.

That's what forgiveness does. It restores our ability to reconnect with one another. Relationships are not perfect. They will run into snags as we hurt and offend one another. As we forgive and are forgiven, we can reconnect.

Fuller Theological Seminary professor Lewis Smedes writes: "Forgiveness is God's invention for coming to terms with a world in which, despite their best intentions, people are unfair to each other and hurt each other deeply. He began by forgiving us. And he invites us all to forgive each other."[34]

8.

COMMUNICATION

A S A PASTOR, one of my busiest days of the week is Sunday. That's why I typically take Mondays off. Often, when I'm not traveling, it is the day I go for an extended run, swim, read my Bible under a favorite tree, have a late lunch with Marie, and we spend the rest of the afternoon together. Usually we'll take in a movie.

On one particular Monday I was hosting a pastor-friend, Bernhard Wewege, who was in town from Christchurch, New Zealand, to consult with me on discipleship. I made arrangements to meet with him in the morning then catch a movie with Marie at five past three.

Because Bernhard wanted to know more about discipleship through relationships, I thought it would be a good idea to demonstrate to him what I meant. After breakfast I brought him to visit a new member of our fellowship, who was the general manager of the five-star Shangri-la Hotel in the city. He and his wife have been growing in their walk with God, and it was a good moment to connect with him while showing my friend how relational discipleship works.

The Shangri-la Hotel is part of a complex that includes a mall and movie theaters that Marie and I frequent, but it is not where we usually go to the movies. Knowing that I was in the hotel, Marie surmised that we would be going to the movie theater at the mall in the complex. Unbeknownst to her, Bernhard was staying at another hotel (the Holiday Inn) that was connected to another mall (The Galleria) not far from where we were at the Shangri-la. Actually, The Galleria is where we typically go to catch a movie.

After the meeting with the executive from church, I drove Bernhard back to his hotel and called Marie to inform her I would hang out at the bookstore in the mall until three then meet up with her in front of the theater. All this time she thought I meant the mall at the Shangri-la complex where Bernhard and I had been earlier that day.

I set my iPhone to buzz fifteen minutes before it was time to meet Marie. I was ten minutes early when I arrived in front of the theater. When she still wasn't there five minutes later, I consoled myself with the fact that we still had ten minutes before the start of the movie. Then it was three, and Marie was still nowhere in sight. I decided to give her a call, thinking she may have been lured by some gigantic sale sign in the mall.

"Where are you?" I asked, trying to be sweet as I filtered my words through the love sieve. "I am standing right in front of the theater," she responded. "Which movie theater?" I inquired. "Number four. You told me you would meet me here," she said. By now I was irritated because I was standing in front of theater number four.

I said, "You can't be standing in front of number four because I am standing in front of it." The sieve did not filter everything. She replied, "Are you telling me I can't read the number four? Of course, I am standing in front of theater number four."

It was then that I had to sense to ask, "Which mall are you in?" She said, "The Shangri-la. Where else would I be?" After more than twenty-eight years of marriage, most of our relational conflicts still stem from a breakdown in communication.

While trust is the foundation of relationships; love is the motive; and forgiveness is what resets, reboots, and restores them, communication is the process by which relationships thrive and grow. This is the fourth building block.

Communication is to a relationship what photosynthesis is to a plant. *Photosynthesis* literally means "photo," or light, that is "synthesized," or "put together." In scientific terms it is the process by which the sun's energy or light converts carbon dioxide and water into energy for the plant. This process of exchange also produces oxygen that is essential to the survival of humans and animals.

Like photosynthesis, communication is the process of exchange that brings people together and produces life in a relationship. Notice how a plant or a tree leans toward the sun, the source of its life. When we have good communication with God and with others, we find that our lives lean in their direction. Just as it is with plants, without "photosynthesis," or communication for the purpose of this discussion, relationships die.

The most basic definition of communication is the sending and receiving of information. It is the successful conveyance and reception of ideas, opinions, and feelings. It's an exchange. And just as photosynthesis is vital to all life on earth, communication is essential to the life of a relationship. A breakdown in communication will result in a breakdown in relationship. In fact, failure in communication was one of the reasons for the downfall of mankind in the Garden of Eden.

BREAKDOWN IN THE GARDEN

> Now the serpent was more crafty than any of the wild animals the LORD God had made. He said to the woman, "Did God really say, '*You must not eat from any tree in the garden?*'"[1]

The breakdown starts imperceptibly. A simple tweak in the communication changed the truth and replaced it with a lie. By simply emphasizing "you must not" rather than "you are free" (which was God's first command), the serpent managed to communicate the wrong message.

God said man was "*free to eat from any tree in the garden.*"[2] The devil said, "Did God really say you '*must not eat from any tree in the garden*'?"[3] He emphasized the restriction rather than the freedom. By using the very same words at the end of the statement, the serpent managed to manipulate the man and woman. The restriction that "you must not eat" was just on one tree, but he managed to make it look like it was on all the trees.

A good liar almost always uses the same words to create the illusion of truth. Partial truth is often more dangerous than an outright lie. That's because it is harder to discern the deception since it has elements of truth in it. Liars know we would be more willing to ingest poison if it tasted familiar.

Here in the garden we see the first element of communication: words. Words are powerful; they are the vehicles by which ideas, opinions, and feelings are conveyed. Notice how Eve responded to the serpent's question.

> The woman said to the serpent, "We may eat fruit from the trees in the garden, but God did say, 'You must not eat fruit from the tree that is in the middle of the garden, and you must not touch it, or you will die.'"[4]

Keep in mind that God initially spoke to Adam, and he was the one responsible for communicating God's word to Eve. Eve's response could have only come from Adam's information, or lack thereof.

This is important to know because Eve's answer was inaccurate. First she said God's restriction was about the tree in the middle of the garden and not about "the tree of the knowledge of good and evil." Secondly, God never said, "You must not touch it." Most important was that she missed out on a vital word when she said, "You will die." God's command included the word "surely."

Now, this might seem like an overreaction to you. After all, Eve understood the gist of the command. But the Bible tells us, "Every word of God is flawless,"[5] and we are commanded to neither add to His words nor take away from them.[6]

Whether she omitted the word herself and added others or Adam failed to communicate what God said accurately to her is something we can only guess. What is for certain from the omission of even the word "surely" is that somehow their communication failed. (You see, our communication issues with our spouses aren't new; they are as old as the Garden of Eden.)

The serpent responded to Eve by saying, "'You will not surely die.... For God knows that when you eat of it your eyes will be opened, and you will be like God, knowing good and evil.'"[7] Communication begins when words are sent. The exchange is completed when the message is received. The woman and the man listened to the serpent, and the communication was completed. Listening is the second part of communication.

Next we read that, "When the woman saw that the fruit of the tree was good for food and pleasing to the eye, and also desirable for gaining wisdom, she took some and ate it. She also gave some to her husband, who was with her, and he ate it."[8]

In this verse we find communication's third element: actions. As the adage goes, "Actions *speak* louder than words." When the woman took the fruit, she communicated to her husband that she was ready to believe the devil's lie. When the man just stood and watched and ate with her without saying a word to stop her, he too communicated his agreement. It was a simple act that changed their destiny.

After Adam and Eve ate of the fruit, "the eyes of both of them were opened, and they realized they were naked; so they sewed fig leaves together and made coverings for themselves. Then the man and his wife *heard the sound of the LORD God* as he was walking in the garden in the cool of the day, and they hid from the LORD God among the trees of the garden."[9]

Notice that the verse above says "the man and his wife heard the sound of the LORD God as he was walking in the cool of the day." With no words or direct actions, God spoke volumes with His mere presence. He was communicating with them through His Spirit. Here we find the most powerful form of communication: spirit. We are spirits that reside in physical bodies, and one of the most powerful forms of communication is the leading of the Holy Spirit.

Our words, listening, actions, and the leading of the Holy Spirit—these are the four elements of communication. Let's look at each one more closely.

EXCHANGING WORDS WITH GOD

The very thought that God wants to communicate with us is mind-boggling. One of the reasons Twitter is so powerful is that it allows regular people to communicate directly with an important or famous individual. People get excited when that celebrity responds to their tweets or mentions them in a comment. Well, God communicates with us directly every day, and He isn't bound by a 140-character limit.

This was the way God originally designed the world to be. There was to be no barrier between us and God. This is what Adam and Eve enjoyed before sin entered the world. I like the way theologian Richard Foster describes the way life was before Adam and Eve's communication encounter with the devil: "In the Garden of Eden Adam and Eve talked with God and God talked with them—they were in communion."[10]

Foster explains that communion with God happens when there is good communication with Him. The good news of the gospel is that God wants to have a relationship with us, and part of that includes communicating with us.

"All good communication in life must begin with communication with God. That's where truth is found."[11] These words of Edwin Louis Cole have been a good reminder to me that before I attempt to develop good communication with anyone, I need to first learn to communicate with God. The way God communicates with us is largely through His Word, and the way we communicate with Him is through prayer.

These two elements of communicating with God are important for us as disciples of Jesus. Reconnecting people with God is our primary objective in discipleship, and people will grow in God as they learn to pray and read their Bible. Author Daniel Henderson writes that "the experience of shared and extended seasons of prayer is a sorely neglected component of real discipleship. Discipleship simply is not sitting at Denny's enjoying a 'Grand Slam' breakfast, filling in the blanks of a booklet. Real discipleship needs to include modeling prayer. Otherwise it is shortsighted."[12]

Only through prayer and studying God's Word will our discipleship produce real, lasting change in people's lives. This is something church leaders of all backgrounds have managed to agree on.

Billy Graham makes two great points to explain the role of the Bible in making disciples. First, he says it is through the reading and study of the Bible that we learn to hear from God.

> Martin Luther was reading his Bible when God spoke to him and it changed the course of history. You come back to the Bible. Begin to read it. Study it and God will speak to you and change you—and through you perhaps history can be changed.[13]

Second, Graham says it is through the preaching and teaching of the Bible that people's lives are transformed.

> I believe that the Bible is a living Word. And I believe that the quoted Word of God is a sword in my hand. If I stick to the Bible and preach the principles and teachings of the Bible, and quote the Bible, it has an impact of its own.[14]

I like the way the late Bible teacher Derek Prince sums up the inter-connectedness of the Bible, discipleship, and our relationship with God.

> The keeping of God's Word is the supreme distinguishing feature, which should mark you out from the world as a disciple of Christ. It is the test of your love for God. It is the cause of God's love and favour toward you. It is the way that Christ will manifest Himself to you. It is the way that God the Father and God the Son will come into your life and make their home with you.[15]

If everyone agrees that we should pray and study God's Word, then why is it so hard for many Christians to do it consistently? Too often when we hear a message about reading our Bible or prayer, we already know what's going to happen. We'll be convinced we need to do it, we'll be convicted for our lack of discipline in this area, and we will resolve to do better next time.

We still approach it as an obligation. But if it's really about a relationship with God, then it should be simple and doable. Our desire to pray and read the Bible should be much like that of someone who is in love. A person in love will read and reread letters from his beloved, and he will spend great lengths of time communicating with that person. It is not a duty but a delight.

The Bible is God's love letter to us, and prayer is simply our way of talking with Him. The New Living Translation of the Bible defines *prayer* well. It is "the most universally practiced yet least understood of human experiences. Prayer is one of the great mysteries of the Christian faith. Its simplest definition is communication with God."[16]

Everything God tells us to do is all about relationship. We aren't fulfilling a quota or doing a chore; we're in a relationship! But by removing prayer and Bible study from the context of relationship, we turn it into an item to put on our spiritual to-do list. We have even gone further and removed prayer from our interaction with one another.

Daniel Henderson explains that "in our culture of rugged individualism we have come to the conclusion that it is better to pray alone than with others. Unfortunately, most of us never learn to do either one very well. Like most disciplines of the Christian faith, we learn best to pray alone when we have been taught in community."[17]

I have great times of prayer on my own, but I also have amazing times with fellow believers. One of the things I learned early in my Christian walk was the value of having lifetime relationships with people who I could pray with. Just the thought of having a fellow believer praying for and with me is an incredible source of encouragement that spurs me to pray for others as well. When we leverage the power of community in prayer, we're getting closer to God's original design.

THE WORD OF GOD IN COMMUNITY

Historically the communication of God's Word was done in the community and in relationships with others. When the Israelites were in the wilderness, the law was read to them as it was given to Moses. The entire community heard the Word of God and confirmed it. The response to the Word of God, whether for celebration or repentance, was also done in community. This continued to the time of the kings and the prophets.

In the New Testament we find Jesus reading the Word of God in the synagogue—with the community. Most of the epistles written by the apostles were meant to be read in front of the church as they gathered. Bill Hull recounts how it was done during the Middle Ages.

> Remember, most people didn't have Bibles, because there were no printing presses. Even if people had Bibles, they wouldn't have been able to read them. However, the reading of Scripture and saying of prayers took place in community worship.[18]

Hull's reason for bringing up this bit of history was to show that at the center of discipleship was the Word of God, despite the unavailability of books. More importantly, he points out that the teaching and study of God's Word was done through relationships in a community.

> Personal devotions, or "quiet time," weren't personal. They were communal out of necessity because the people couldn't read or write....While we don't want to idealize the people who lived during those days, we certainly should look at how discipleship was alive and well in that process. And we should be brave enough to admit that perhaps one reason so many present-day

disciples struggle to do devotions alone is that they are best done in community.[19]

Discipleship then as it is now must be centered on the written Word of God. Its reading, discussion, study, application, and prayer are still best done in relationship with other believers.

"Learn to Play Ping-Pong"

Words are just the first part of communication. Listening is just as important, as any wife can attest. Marie often comments that I do not listen to her very well. In the past she also complained that when the discussion was a topic right up my alley, I often talked too much and did not allow her to speak.

Fortunately I married a wise and loving woman. She once told me, "Joey, you need to learn to play Ping-Pong. Talking to people is like playing Ping-Pong. You have to hit the ball and then let the other person hit the ball back to you. No one will want to play with you if you're the only one hitting the ball. You can't expect people to just keep picking up the balls you hit."

I fought the temptation to tell her that preventing the other person from hitting the ball back was exactly the goal of table tennis. But her word picture made sense because I knew how tiring it was to keep picking up the balls people send your way, especially those that go out of bounds.

It has been many years since Marie gave me this word picture. It has helped me literally bite my tongue on many occasions, so I could do a better job of listening and not cut people off with my ideas. Admittedly I still have lapses.

Over time I learned how to "play Ping-Pong." Although I must admit that I still slam those balls with an occasional drive, Marie graciously acknowledges that I have improved. Marie's word picture not only saved our marriage, but it also made me realize the importance of good listening skills. Communication is an exchange. It does not flow only one way.

We read in the Book of James, "My dear brothers, take note of this: Everyone should be *quick to listen*, slow to speak and slow to become angry."[20] In this verse James focuses not only on being "quick to listen" but also on being "slow to speak," or being silent in order to hear better.

Real listening is allowing the person to speak his heart and mind without our interpreting, evaluating, or guiding his thoughts to align with ours. This creates empathy that builds relationships as we truly share in what a person is saying. It allows us to give and receive ministry more effectively.

In their book *Coaching 101*, Robert Logan and Sherilyn Carlton explain the significance of listening this way:

> It is the essential cornerstone of every relationship. How do you get to know someone? By listening. How do you build trust? By listening. How do you help people think through their goals, their opinions, their feelings? By listening. People want to know they are being heard."[21]

We disciple people by building relationships with them, and one of the ways we do this is by listening to them. Often what we call listening is not really listening. That's because we already know what we're going to say after the person speaks. We're merely waiting for them to finish so we can speak.

When we listen, we will hear the person's heart and know how best to respond and minister to him. There is no better listener than God Himself. Notice how His first four sets of words to Adam and Eve were in the form of questions? He did this so He could listen to them. Listening allows us to know what is in people's hearts.

ACTIONS SPEAK

When Marie and I first became Christians back in the mid-eighties, a neighbor invited us to attend a small group Bible study. It was there where we met Deng and Sucel (pronounced Suzelle) Samonte, who taught us so much more with their lives than with their words.

Back then our children were very young, and they would distract us during our small group meetings (imagine three boys!). Deng and Sucel came up with a remedy a few meetings later. They brought their two daughters (who were just a few years older than our sons) to take charge of childcare. That one act of service taught us more about kindness and love than any teaching they gave.

When they did teach, it wasn't done with much pedagogical skill. Often they really did not teach but asked questions and patiently allowed us to draw our own conclusions about God's Word.

They also taught us how to pray. Their commitment to prayer was evident every time we met. Silently inviting the presence of God and tuning their spiritual ears to hear what He was saying, they led our group as they were led by the Holy Spirit.

Outside the meetings they visited those who needed more care. There was the couple whose life was met with persistent challenges because of the wife's long-term illness. Deng and Sucel stood and encouraged them. And when she passed away, they continued to encourage her husband to follow Christ. We also witnessed how they reached out to our neighbors who were steeped in substance abuse. They even made time for us.

These expressions of love and care took place more than twenty years ago, and yet the lessons we learned from them have stayed with us to this day. Their actions spoke louder than their words. It is as Daniel Henderson wrote, "Our messages tell people what to do. Our lives show them how to do it."[22]

Often what astonishes people about our God is not what we say but what they see: our actions. Hence we are encouraged by the words of the apostle John, "Dear children, let us not love with words or tongue but with actions and in truth."[23]

I recently caught up with Deng and Sucel in Los Angeles. Since they led our small Bible study, they have become missionaries to the City of Angels. Sucel serves in a local church while Deng works in nursing homes ushering the elderly into eternity. Again their actions often communicate more than their words.

Communicating with our actions can sometimes be even more powerful than communicating with our words. As Bill Hull has said, "The people who love you and whom you trust have incredible power and influence over you."[24]

Keep in mind that according to UNESCO (United Nations Educational, Scientific, and Cultural Organization), millions of people around the world remain illiterate.[25] Much of what people will see as the Word of

God are the loving relationships they experience as they are lived out by God's people.

PREVAILED UPON BY THE SPIRIT

Some years back I was invited to speak on discipleship by a pastor friend from Dallas. In training his leaders, I went on site to be with a group of students at Southern Methodist University. The goal was to model how small group discipleship worked.

As we sat in the room, I asked the group what their greatest challenge for the week was. It was my way of breaking the ice and warming things up. Each person discussed a trial they faced. For one it was pressure from coming exams; for another it was just the "busyness" of life. Others followed with trials ranging from not being able to do the laundry to simply just missing home.

Then a young woman said, "I've been thinking of my father who was diagnosed with cancer." As I sat in the room, I felt the Holy Spirit whisper something like, "Pause the meeting and focus on her." I thought to myself, "I came all the way from the Philippines to train these guys. I shouldn't get distracted but should focus on the business at hand."

Fortunately the Holy Spirit prevailed. I asked the woman a series of questions about her father. They were simple questions such as: Where is he? How old is he? What stage is the cancer? I patiently listened to her plight and noticed that the other people in the room were being touched by the Holy Spirit along with her.

They came expecting to see a discipleship program; what they saw instead was a real-life demonstration of how discipleship relationships work. The people started to empathize with her. Some feeling her emotions even cried with her.

For a while we turned the meeting into a short time of prayer. We prayed for her and for the other challenges expressed. I share this story to underscore a vitally important point: our words, listening, and actions are for naught without the power and presence of the Holy Spirit.

Not all small group meetings are as dramatic as this one. God's presence is not always predicated by some emotional, exciting, and unexpected event. Rather it is wrapped in righteousness, peace, and joy,[26] something that can be experienced by everyone in all our small group meetings.

In his book *The Life You've Always Wanted* John Ortberg explains what it is like to be sensitive to the Holy Spirit.

> Consider the difference between piloting a motorboat or a sailboat. We can run a motorboat all by ourselves. We can fill the tank and start the engine. We are in control. But a sailboat is a different story. We can hoist the sails and steer the rudder, but we are utterly dependent on the wind. The wind does the work. If the wind doesn't blow—and sometimes it doesn't—we sit still in the water no matter how frantic we act. Our task is to do whatever enables us to catch the wind.[27]

Jesus said, "The wind blows wherever it pleases. You hear its sound, but you cannot tell where it comes from or where it is going. So it is with everyone born of the Spirit."[28] To say discipleship is relationship means whether we're studying the Bible, praying, listening, or responding, our communication must be led and controlled by the Holy Spirit. It is His ministry that touches, transforms, heals, and comforts people. Ultimately it is His ministry that causes people to receive Christ as Lord. We are utterly dependent on Him. Before we can effectively communicate with others, we must learn to communicate with Him.

THE LAST BUILDING BLOCK

This chapter does not purport to define communication. Neither is it about how to improve one's skills in communicating. Rather it is an attempt at explaining the role communication has in discipleship relationships. It starts with communicating with God through prayer, the consistent reading and interaction with His Word, the Bible. It's about learning to listen to the Holy Spirit, to other believers, and to those whom we are led to grow in discipleship with. It is also about our actions and the way our spirit communicates, often without us even realizing it.

When we pray and read His Word, we interface with God. This constant action will result in the continual growth of our understanding and trust of God. We are able to better grasp how wide and long, how high and deep is His love for us in Christ Jesus. We are humbled by the consistency of His mercy and forgiveness that are new every morning.

Communicating with God means communing with Him. When we do, we imbibe His Spirit. The result is that we communicate not just lessons; we literally impart a spirit of trust, love, and forgiveness to those we are in discipleship with. And just as we have pointed out in the previous chapter, all three are found in Christ's blood. When we are covered and washed by nothing but the revelation of the shed blood of Christ, we will naturally impart all three to those around us.

And as the writer of Hebrews points out, it is also Christ's "sprinkled blood that speaks a better word than the blood of Abel."[29]

"All by Itself"

As I end this chapter, let me summarize the four essentials of a healthy relationship: trust, love, forgiveness, and communication. Like a child who grows naturally when she is healthy, relationships grow "automatically" when these four essentials are present.

When telling His disciple a parable about a seed that sprouted and grew, Jesus said, "All by itself the soil produces grain—first the stalk, then the head, then the full kernel in the head."[30] Christian Schwarz, who has written about church growth strategies, explains what Jesus meant by the phrase "all by itself."

> Most commentators agree that this "by itself" is the key for understanding this parable. Just what does it mean? The term used in the Greek is "automate"—literally translated it means "automatic."[31]

Schwarz uses this parable to make the point that some things become automatic when all the right elements combine together. This is true of relationships. When the four ingredients of trust, love, forgiveness, and communication are present, our discipleship relationships will grow naturally "all by itself."

In his book *LEGO: A Love Story* Jonathan Bender chronicles the activities of "Adult Fans of LEGO" (AFOL). These fans, ranging from ages twenty to well into the forties, still build and play with LEGO, and they are the purest of the purists. That means they will use only original LEGO pieces.

Today there are other companies that have copied LEGO. If LEGO bricks and other bricks are mixed in a pile, one would have a hard time figuring out which is a LEGO brick and which isn't. Not AFOL members. They have developed a way to determine which is which when working with a pile of varied pieces. It's called the "drop test."

If they suspect that a brick is not original, they simply drop it on a tabletop. The sound instantly tells them if it's the real McCoy or not. Fake pieces sound hollow; LEGO pieces have a more solid sound.

Jesus said, "For out of the overflow of his heart his mouth speaks."[32] In a way we're like LEGO bricks. When we build on the Word of God as our foundation, our lives and words will have a depth that will sound solid to those around us.

SECTION III

VALUES

9.

BRICK BY BRICK

Y OU LEFT A career as a highly paid corporate lawyer to become a LEGO artist?" The question was posed by one of America's favorite talk-show hosts, Stephen Colbert of *The Colbert Report*. His guest that evening was Nathan Sawaya, a New York attorney who had, in fact, left his job to become a LEGO brick sculptor.

"I wanted to follow my passion," Nathan said calmly. "My passion was being an artist." To this Stephen countered, "Being an artist or being a little boy?" Then came laughter from the audience.

"I enjoy being an artist, and that was much better than being a lawyer," Nathan responded. Stephen continued to tease him: "Adulthood is about doing what you need to do not what you enjoy." The audience tittered.

Nathan smiled. "I find that you can be successful at doing the things you enjoy." Stephen then challenged him with, "Do people pay for your art?" Nathan replied, "They do. They actually pay money for my art."

"How much would someone pay for art made of LEGO?" Stephen asked incredulously while taking a sip of water.

"Twenty to thirty thousand dollars." With perfect comedic timing Stephen spurted out the water in his mouth exclaiming, "Wow, I did not expect that."

What can we glean from Nathan's story? He left a high-paying career in order to do what he enjoyed and followed his passion. Jonathan Bender writes about Nathan's early days as a LEGO artist: "He became an instant media sensation: nobody leaves his job as a corporate lawyer to get paid $13 an hour to build with LEGO bricks."[1]

What we enjoy and are passionate about, we value. What we value, we willingly sacrifice for. But there's another aspect of Nathan's story that I wish to bring to our attention: seemingly insignificant bricks connected together by a master become art pieces of high value. Similarly, our lives placed in Jesus's hands and joined together in discipleship relationships become extraordinary communities of high value.

Just to give a quick recap: We began this book by talking about discipleship. We said that this is God's mission for the church. It's the one thing we need to focus on that ties the Christian life together. We also saw that discipleship is relationship.

We then examined the four elements of relationship—trust, love, forgiveness, and communication. These are the building blocks that make relationships work. We saw how these broke down when Adam and Eve first sinned and how salvation through Jesus Christ is the only way we can be restored relationally to God. Now to round out this picture of discipleship as relationship, let's examine the concept of value.

WHY VALUES?

You may be wondering why I'd want to dedicate an entire section of a book on discipleship to the subject of values. The answer is actually quite simple—because values are about the heart, as Jesus said, "For where *your treasure* is, there *your heart* will be also."[2]

What we value (treasure) is an indicator of the true condition of our hearts. Here are a few examples:

- When I don't read my Bible and pray on certain days, it is an indicator that I have valued another activity more than God and His Word.

- Taking my wife for granted only means I have valued something more than my relationship with her.

- When I snap at my children and become impatient, it simply shows that at that moment my convenience is more valuable to me than them.

- When being right is more important than engaging the people I meet, I have valued my time (sometimes my insecurity) more than having a relationship with others.

- When I'm always late for church but am always on time for the movies, it shows that entertainment is more valuable to me than the things of God.

If discipleship is relationship, then it cannot be about a program but about the heart, hence this section on values.

While some see Western Christianity as declining, I'm in the school of thought that believes true Christianity is burgeoning even as cultural Christianity wanes. But to see this growing shift expand, changes need to be made. The starting point is a change in values. This is because values deal with the heart, and without a change of heart there is no chance of any lasting change.

A shift in the trend will depend largely on how what Christians value changes. By values I do not mean the statements we plaster on church walls and print in bulletins. In the simplest of terms, what I mean by values is *that which is most important.*

As long as we value comfort and convenience, money and material things over our relationship with God and people, nothing much will change. I am convinced this was the problem the Pharisees had—wrong values and wrong hearts, which equals no change. We see this truth played out in what I call Jesus's most confusing parable.

JESUS'S MOST CONFUSING PARABLE

Of all Jesus's parables the one about the dishonest manager has been the most confusing to me. As the story goes, the manager was accused of wasting his master's possessions. When asked to give an accounting of his transactions, he dishonestly manipulated the situation to protect himself.[3] Then Jesus puts an unexpected twist to the story:

> The master *commended the dishonest manager* because he had acted shrewdly. For the people of this world are more shrewd in dealing with their own kind than are the people of the light.[4]

Did I read that right? If the master is God, did He just commend the dishonest manager? Yes, He did. But what's important to understand is that while the master commended the dishonest manager, the commendation was not for his dishonesty.

There's no telling how many commentaries I have read to make sense of this parable. What has thrown me off all these years are the titles that have been given to the parable, usually either "The Dishonest Manager" or "The Unjust Steward." The first title has led me to think the parable was about honesty. The second one made me think it was about stewardship.

But even after many years of reading the text, I still wasn't clear about what the parable was saying. Only when I read the parable again through the lens of relationships and values did I see a perspective that may help us understand it better.

In Luke 16 we find the manager contemplating his situation. Let's take a closer look:

> The manager said to himself, "What shall I do now? My master is taking away my job. I'm not strong enough to dig, and I'm ashamed to beg—I know what I'll do so that, when I lose my job here, people will welcome me into their houses."[5]

Realizing the seriousness of his predicament, he shrewdly and strategically strengthens his relationship with his master's debtors.

> So he called in each one of his master's debtors. He asked the first, "*How much* do you owe my master?" "Eight hundred gallons of olive oil," he replied. The manager told him, "Take your bill, sit down quickly, and make it four hundred." Then he asked the second, "And how much do you owe?" "A thousand bushels of wheat," he replied. He told him, "Take your bill and make it eight hundred."[6]

Clearly the discussion involved weights, measures, and values. But the reason for the commendation was not his dishonesty but his foresight to realize that in this world relationships matter—a lot. Since there was no way to keep the relationship with his master, he could at least strengthen his relationship with his other associates. The result was that "the master commended the dishonest manager because he had acted shrewdly. For the people of this world are *more shrewd* in dealing with their own kind *than are the people of the light.*"[7]

Not only was the man commended for understanding the importance of relationships, but his actions were also contrasted with that of Christians ("people of the light"), who often focus on doing things "business as usual" without realizing how important building and maintaining relationships are. The next verse explains what the commendation was about:

> I tell you, *use worldly wealth to gain friends* for yourselves, so that when it is gone, you will be welcomed into eternal dwellings.[8]

Notice how the discussion focuses on worldly wealth (values) and gaining friends (relationships). No doubt the dishonest manager is manipulating people, yet Jesus still uses this negative example as an encouragement to us to build true friendships. Undoubtedly this parable was about values and relationships.

Jesus was instructing His disciples to use whatever things of value we have to gain friends and win them over. And just as the manager was welcomed by these friends, those whom we reach in this world will also welcome us in our eternal dwellings. Ultimately what is of eternal value is our relationships with God and with people.

To ensure His listeners didn't make the mistake of concluding that He was condoning dishonesty, Jesus clarified His position in the next verse:

> Whoever can be trusted with very little can also be trusted with much, and whoever is dishonest with very little will also be dishonest with much.[9]

After clarifying the issue of honesty, Jesus further underscored the point about the connection between values and relationships by saying:

> So if you have not been trustworthy in handling worldly wealth, who will trust you with true riches?[10]

Jesus's point was amazing. If you don't know how to value your relationships over wealth, who will entrust you with what is truly valuable, which, as we will see later, includes people's souls.

WRONG VALUES

After Jesus told this parable, we find the Pharisees reacting to His teaching: "The Pharisees, *who loved money*, heard all this and were sneering at Jesus."[11]

They scoffed because they had a faulty value system. They valued money over relationship with God and people. This is where we find the essence of the parable and the real lesson behind the story.

> He said to them, "You are the ones who justify yourselves in the eyes of men, but *God knows your hearts*. What is *highly valued* among men is detestable in God's sight."[12]

Here again we see the connection between our hearts and what we value. Jesus points out an obvious thing that is easy to miss—what we value is very different from what God values. More accurately, what we highly value is often detestable to God. And what did the Pharisees love or highly value? Money.

Money is powerful. It has the ability to buy position, power, protection, and provision. It could purchase slaves, buy friends, overthrow governments, and sway the masses. Money has taken the place of all the ancient gods. Those who have lots of it could, for all intents and purposes, be like "living gods." All the other gods are paid lip service, but men truly give their trust, love, and hearts to money.

Money has become the god of this world. This is why Jesus singled it out as the one that could compete with God for our hearts.

> No one can serve two masters. Either he will hate the one and love the other, or he will be devoted to the one and despise the other. You cannot serve both God and Money.[13]

When economic downturns hit nations and regions, the response of the people reveal just how much they were trusting in money as their practical god. Could God be allowing such things to happen in the world because He will have no other gods before Him?

It is vital to see the difference between God and money. The chart below compares the two.

GOD	MONEY
Sets us free	Controls and manipulates
Satisfies completely	Does not fully satisfy
Is unlimited	Is limited
Reveals the truth	Deceives
Is eternal	Is temporal

Keep in mind that Judas's act of treachery was not a simple matter of disloyalty but of misplaced values that involved money.

> Then one of the Twelve—the one called Judas Iscariot—went to the chief priests and asked, "What are you willing to give me if I hand him over to you?" So they counted out for him thirty silver coins.[14]

Money controlled and manipulated Judas. It did not satisfy him. It was limited in its ability to save him. And it deceived him into going for the temporal. Judas could not take the silver coins with him. There are, however, two things of eternal value we can take with us to eternity when we die.

What You Can Take With You

Jesus told His disciples, "Do not store up for yourselves treasures on earth, where moth and rust destroy, and where thieves break in and steal."[15] Growing up you may have heard people say, "You can't take it with you." We've heard preachers declare, "You never see a U-Haul behind a hearse." Both statements are meant to warn us not to store for ourselves treasures on earth, because we can't take them with us beyond the grave.

These statements, however, are incomplete. Jesus actually said we could store up treasures in heaven.

But *store up for yourselves treasures in heaven*, where moth and rust do not destroy, and where thieves do not break in and steal.[16]

The big question is, what treasures can we take to heaven? Gold is equivalent to asphalt in heaven. Pearls are what gates are made of in Paradise Lane. So what kind of treasure can we take with us, the one that is valued in heaven?

Of all that is in heaven, God is the number one value, and the second is people. If people are valuable in heaven, it stands to reason that they are valuable on earth too.

So what is the treasure that will welcome us in heaven? People. Friends who will thank and welcome you for being a part of their life and leading them to Christ. So what are the two things of eternal value we can take with us? Our relationship with God and our relationships with people.

Consider Francis Schaeffer's take on values and people:

All men bear the image of God. They have value, not because they are redeemed, but because they are God's creation in God's image. Modern man who has rejected this, has no clue as to who he is, and because of this he can find no real value for himself or for other men. Hence, he downgrades the value of other men and produces the horrible thing we face today—a sick culture in which men treat men as inhuman, as machines.

As Christians, however, we know the value of men. All men are our neighbors, and we are to love them as ourselves. We are to do this on the basis of creation, even if they are not redeemed, for all men have value because they are made in the image of God. Therefore they are to be loved even at great cost.[17]

Jesus not only underscores the value of people, but He also affirms that every single person is valuable. The parable of the lost sheep highlights the depth to which God values each person.

What do you think? If a man owns a hundred sheep, and *one* of them wanders away, will he not leave the ninety-nine on the hills and go to look for *the one* that wandered off?[18]

In this parable Jesus made it clear that to God every single person is important; each one is valuable. No one is too small, too insignificant, too lost, too far off, too different, too indifferent, too young, too old, too sinful, too proud, too rich, too poor, too clean, or too dirty—everyone is valuable.

And like Nathan Sawaya, who built his LEGO masterpieces brick by brick, eventually creating structures worth thousands of dollars, we also can build toward the greatest goal of all—the discipling of all nations, one person at a time. And we are even more motivated than Nathan to value the individual, because while he works with plastic bricks, we are entrusted with the pinnacle of God's creation—human beings who bear His image.

This is why we all need to be mobilized in making disciples. The sheer number and variety of people will require every disciple of Christ to actively engage the people they know. Valuing each person is the key.

Jesus continues His parable about the lost sheep by saying, "And if he finds it, I tell you the truth, *he is happier* about that *one sheep* than about the ninety-nine that did not wander off."[19] This is what brings God happiness, for this is what He values—people, every single one of them.

The parable ends with Jesus saying the Father is not willing to let anyone be lost: "In the same way your Father in heaven is not willing that *any of these little ones* should be lost."[20] I pray that the Holy Spirit will open our eyes and hearts to share this value that is most important to Him. Every person is valuable. And more than that God desires that each person be sought after.

Indeed "the harvest is plentiful, but the workers are few."[21] When we as followers of Christ embrace this value and apply this principle, we will see an exponential growth in discipleship and the unabated expansion of the kingdom of God.

DISCIPLESHIP AND VALUES

Kevin York, the executive director of Every Nation Ministries (the church movement I am privileged to be a part of), made a simple statement that helps explain the discipleship and values connection. He said, "As long as you aim for your values, you will most likely hit your vision, mission, and programs."

He explained that having discipleship as our main value allows us to come up with the right processes, vision, mission, and programs. Many discipleship ventures fizzle out in churches and among Christians because they are vision-based, mission-focused, and program-driven rather than being about values.

While these three are vital and important, all are subject to change; values rarely do. Dallas Seminary Professor Aubrey Malphurs explains it this way:

> Values are constant. Values are tenacious. Like barnacles attached to the hull of a ship they tend to hang on tightly.... While values do change, they do not change easily and quickly.[22]

Clearly, values are the more powerful agent. They influence everything: vision, mission focus, programs, and methods. Best-selling authors James Collins and Jerry Porras write about values and their consistent and unchanging nature. "Core values need no rational or external justification," they say. "Nor do they sway with the trends and fads of the day."[23]

We don't determine our values by listing nice thoughts on a paper and voting on them. We already have values in our hearts. Our everyday actions—where we spend our resources, what makes us happy or sad, what we notice in situations—reveal what is most important to us.

Some people confuse values with principles. A principle is a fundamental truth or proposition that serves as the foundation for a system of belief or behavior or for a chain of reasoning, such as the basic principles of Christianity. It can also mean a rule or belief governing one's personal behavior or morally correct behavior and attitudes, which is what is meant by the expression "a man of principle."

Based on these definitions, we can see the word *principle* has to do with a system of belief, a way of doing life, and our behavior and attitudes. But as fundamental as they are, principles still come from somewhere. They were created as an outworking of a preexisting set of values. It is values that shape principles. Let me explain.

- Financial principles are based on monetary and gold values.

- Corporate principles are based on its founders' and boards' values.

- Marketing principles are shaped by customer values.

- Christian principles are founded on what God values.

As important as principles are, they are not the starting point; values are. People may know the principles to good health but will only apply them to the degree that they value their lives and their bodies. Couples may know the principles to a good marriage but will only practice them if they value their relationship. This is also true of discipleship. One may know what the principles of discipleship are, but he will live them out only if he shares God's values.

Ultimately, the LEGO Principle boils down to a question of values. If we don't value what God values, then these principles for discipleship serve us no purpose. But if we have His heart, the principles work themselves out in our lives.

When we value people, we will engage them with the intent of leading them to Christ. When we know how valuable Jesus is to our lives and to others, we will establish new believers in the foundation of Christ. When we understand the strategic value of ministry, we will equip every believer to minister. Finally, as we learn to value each day of our lives, we will empower all disciples to make disciples.

VALUE	PRINCIPLE
People are valuable	Engage your community and culture
Jesus is most valuable	Establish believers in the foundation of Christ
Ministry is valuable	Equip every believer to minister
Every day is valuable	Empower all disciples to make disciples

In the next four chapters we will look at each of these values and the corresponding discipleship principle that applies to them.

The LEGO company has been in operation since 1932. It has weathered worldwide upheavals and undergone many changes and transitions. What is remarkable is that LEGO has remained a privately held company owned by the Christiansen family.

Unlike other toy companies that have changed owner-ship, LEGO has enjoyed eighty years of operating under the same values of its original founders. While their product lines, manufacturing practices, and marketing initiatives have changed, their values have remained the same.

Similarly throughout history the church has gone through many challenges and revolutions. Methods and styles of ministry have come and gone. Where the church has erred, we can see that it started with a divergence from the heart of God. Conversely, where the church has seen lasting fruit has been in the times when it was building according to God's values.

10.

PEOPLE ARE VALUABLE

MY SECOND-BORN SON, David, is the businessman of the family. He has a degree in economics and a good grasp of what creates value. David's understanding is not merely academic. He grew up with an uncanny ability to appreciate goods that are of high quality. As a little boy, when he spotted a car he liked on the road, he would point to it and say, "I like that car," not knowing its make or model. Often he would be pointing to a BMW, Jaguar, or Mercedes Benz though we never owned a European car.

When he was eight, I brought him with me on one of my business trips. When we dined at a pricey restaurant, he instinctively found the most expensive soup, appetizer, and main course. As a teenager who played tennis, when choosing from an array of racquets he always managed to pick the most expensive from among the lot. To his credit it was usually the one that was best made.

Over time David grew up to take on more of his heavenly Father's values. His concerns evolved from well-designed cars, expensive hors d'oeuvres, and the latest evolution of tennis racquets. Today David serves as a member of the board of directors of Habitat for Humanity in the Philippines. He actively feeds very poor children and helps provide educational scholarships through the Real Life Foundation as a volunteer. David also loves God with a passion and is an avid disciple maker. All this he does while remaining a businessman.

I credit David for helping me navigate the relationship between discipleship and values. Being a businessman, David constantly engages me on the subject of values, and his insights have been invaluable. One of our conversations led us to how one measures the intrinsic value of products and services such as cars, watches, and hotel rooms. How does one measure the differences in worth between one car and another, a gold watch and one that is plastic, a stay at a five-star hotel versus budget accommodations?

I argued that a European sports coupe and a Korean-made car will eventually arrive at the same destination, a gold watch and one made of plastic will tell the same time, and at the end of the day a hotel room is a bed, a bath, and a toilet. He grinned at me and said, "You're thinking too much like a pastor." David knows that as a pastor I drive a Ford SUV. I don't own a watch (and tell time from my iPhone) and can't afford luxury hotels.

He reasoned that not all cars, watches, and hotel rooms are equal. Some are more valuable than others. A Ferrari is not the same as a Kia. A Rolex is not a Timex, and staying at a Four Seasons does not compare with lodging at a Days Inn. The increase in value comes from the kind of materials used, the design and craftsmanship, and the experience its users receive.

He explained that Ferrari, Rolex, and the Four Seasons do not settle for anything less than the best materials. Whether the material is steel, leather, gold, diamonds, bed sheets, or soap, it must conform to the highest standards. High-quality goods and services are made of items that are a cut above—"specialty-alloy" metal, "hand-sewn" leather, "refined" eighteen-karat gold, "flawless" diamonds.

Those high-end goods and services are also associated with premium suppliers such as Frette and La Prairie. Together they increase the intrinsic value of these products and services.

But Ferraris, Rolexes, and even the Four Seasons are not just about materials. Their design and craftsmanship add significantly to their value. These products combine function with beauty, durability with symmetry, and harmony with excellence in design and craftsmanship. Combined they give their users an experience they cherish and, yes, value.

Another important point in understanding value is that the rarer or more uncommon the substance or product is, the more valuable it becomes. Leather is less common than vinyl. A diamond is rarer than crystal. Soaps made from organically grown herbs are not as common as ones manufactured chemically. Ferrari, Rolex, and the Four Seasons combine materials, design, and craftsmanship that are "rarer" than their counterparts and as such make their products and services more valuable.

Finally the robustness, durability, shelf life, and duration of a product or service also add value. Stainless steel is more resistant to corrosion and tarnishing. Gold is what heirlooms are made of. Memories of stays at the Four Seasons are said to last a lifetime.

The reason our world operates on intrinsic values is because much of God's creation functions the same way. The only difference is God does not value inanimate objects as much as we do. God values people so much more.

SOME THINGS DON'T COMPARE

David went on to explain that if you lined up a Ferrari, Rolex, and a monthlong stay at the Four Seasons and compared them to a human being (even one who has many strikes against him in your mind), pound for pound that person will have a greater intrinsic value than any of those material things.

Just consider the marvelous way our bodies work. Compared to a Ferrari, Rolex, or the luxury features at the Four Seasons, our bodies are far more beautiful, complex, rare, and amazing. The psalmist came to the same conclusion as my son did when he said, "I praise you because I am fearfully and wonderfully made; your works are wonderful, I know that full well."[1]

Think about our body's ability to protect and maintain itself. The intricacies of our eyes are more complex than any microscope ever developed. Robotic research has yet to come up with hands whose dexterity compares with ours. An alliance between Apple, IBM, and Microsoft would be hard pressed to invent a supercomputer that can come close to functioning the way our brains do. Even at birth a baby's brain contains one million million (1,000,000,000,000) brain cells, or neurons.[2]

And what about our hearts—the tiniest, quietest pump of its kind that runs 24/7 moving liters of liquid perpetually while incredibly powered by a small amount of nutrition in the form of grains, fruits, proteins, and water? Then think of the design of our circulatory, digestive, immune, respiratory, and reproductive systems. What craftsmanship and attention to detail. The strands of hair, nails, skin, muscles, capillaries, and bones not only grow but also replenish and even heal themselves, and they are all assembled in perfect harmony and work together as one. It is simply amazing!

When it comes to being rare, God has created such a variety of people that each has his own distinct intrinsic value. We are of different races, shapes, sizes, and colors, and we are each so rare that no two human beings have the same set of fingerprints.

INDEFINITE SHELF LIFE

When I wrote this chapter in 2010, I was in Camp John Hay, a resort in the city of Baguio in the Philippines. With its rolling hills, beautiful landscape, and perfect weather, Baguio is a good place to write. After a run one morning, I walked around the resort to cool down. I then found myself alongside an elderly woman.

I greeted her with a polite "good morning," and she responded in kind. I asked her if she worked at the resort, and she replied, "Oh, no, I'm too old. But I grew up in this land. My ancestors lived at the foot of this hill long before the Americans came and turned it into a rest and recreation camp for their military personnel in the region. Eventually I worked for them. I'm now retired, but I love walking here every day."

After we exchanged names, I asked her how old she was. I couldn't have been more surprised by her answer. She looked at me and said, "I was born in 1908. That makes me 102 years old."

My jaw nearly dropped as she looked like she was in her early sixties—and she was keeping pace with me uphill and down! I wanted to know her secret, and she said, "I walk every day, avoid worrying, and eat a lot of sweet potatoes."

Later in the conversation she asked what I did, and I told her I was a pastor. This allowed me to ask her if she knew Jesus. "Yes," she said, "the American missionaries taught us about Him, and my pastor reminds me of Him every week."

The shelf life of the average human being is seventy years, though for some, like my new friend, it is a little longer. More important, though, is that part of what gives a human being his intrinsic value is a soul made in the image of our very own Creator. At this level shelf life lasts indefinitely.

Jesus posed this question to His disciples to highlight the value of a human soul: "What can a man give in exchange for his soul?"[3]

My encounter with the woman reminded me of my son's insights on the value of humans. As the woman and I said good-bye, I lifted up a prayer for her. Then I thought of how often we miss out on unique experiences like this one because we haven't learned to value one another more. One thing is for sure, I will surely try to take longer walks every day, worry less, and eat more sweet potatoes!

Seeing things from this perspective is what will help believers unravel, demystify, and overcome one of the most difficult and challenging aspects of our walk with God—sharing our faith with others. The reason we don't reach out to others is not because we don't know that we should. And it's not because we don't know how, because we will gladly learn anything we truly value knowing. The honest and difficult truth is that we just don't value people as much as we value material things.

Unless our values perspective changes and we see every human being's worth from God's eyes, not much will happen in terms of evangelism. When we get our values straight we will freely reach out and apply the first principle of discipleship.

PRINCIPLE 1: ENGAGE YOUR COMMUNITY AND CULTURE

One of the things that intimidate Christians is being told they should evangelize their friends and relations. Many feel unprepared for the possible questions and the rejection that may result. That's because we have reduced evangelism to a sales pitch that demands that people make a decision rather than engaging non-Christians through relationships. A relationship that develops over time can lead people to know Jesus as their Savior. Think about it: even Jesus spent thirty years engaging earth before He started to make disciples.

It was pastor Steve Murrell who I first heard challenge Christians to engage our community and culture. Steve constantly points out that Jesus's disciples interpreted His Great Commission to mean they should find people who were not yet followers of Jesus and help them to know and follow Him. He points out that it is when we disconnect engaging community and culture from discipleship that we disenfranchise multitudes from effectively being the disciple makers they were meant to be. The result is that very little engaging of people occurs.

Bear in mind that Jesus's commission was to go "into all the world" and not "into all the churches." Besides, when Jesus issued His commission to go and make disciples, there were no churches. Discipleship meant His followers first had to find people who did not believe and engage them. In our present context this can also mean people who are born into Christianity culturally but are not disciples of Jesus.

Discipleship does not start when people give their lives to Christ and come to church. It begins long before that when Christ's disciples engage them in a relationship. Jesus's call for us to make disciples of all nations was not a pipe dream or an unattainable delusion, but a command that could be accomplished if all His followers would simply obey Him.

Unfortunately, if there was any engaging being done, it may have been sending the wrong signals. The book *unChristian* is based on years of in-depth research by David Kinnaman and Gabe Lyons, and it shows that Christians often send the wrong vibe to those outside the church.

> Our most recent data show that young outsiders have lost much of their respect for the Christian faith. These days nearly two out of every five young outsiders (38 percent) claim to have a bad impression of present-day Christianity....We are known for having an us-versus-them mentality. Outsiders believe Christians do not like them because of what they do, how they look, or what they believe. They feel minimized—or worse, demonized—by those who love Jesus.[4]

These results are not due to one church or denomination. Christians of every stripe are guilty of alienating people who are not from their so-called "Christian bubble." The problem is so pervasive I sometimes wonder if a mutated form of xenophobia against sinners is spreading among Christians. As Kinnaman and Lyons point out, "We have become famous for what we oppose, rather than who we are."[5]

What can be done about this? Steve Murrell has been telling us for years: "Engage your community and culture."

To *engage* means to attract someone's interest. Thus we say we have engaged someone's attention when they participate in or become curious about something—a book, for example, or an activity or a cause. Yet to engage also means to make a significant or meaningful connection, like a couple who is engaged to be married.

Second, our *community* is those immediately around us: our family, friends, neighbors, work associates, and those we come in contact with.

Last, *culture* is comprised of the things we do without thinking. Culture is about how we act and communicate. It is largely formed by the person's values and ultimately becomes his behavior, language, and the overall demeanor that marks him. It also consists of where we live, work, shop, and play. In short, culture reveals what we value and enjoy.

Therefore to engage our community and culture means to attract the interest and make a significant connection with our relatives, friends, and all the other people groups we come into contact with every day. It's time for Christianity to regain its lost luster—to become "famous" for the right reason: Jesus.

CNN's Hero of the Year

In November 2009 Filipinos everywhere were glued to their television sets waiting to find out who would be named CNN's Hero of the Year. The Blue Ribbon Panel tasked with selecting the winner included Gen. Colin Powell, philanthropist Wallis Annenberg, businessman Ted Turner, former LA Lakers coach Phil Jackson, and singer Elton John, among others. CNN had launched the annual award with a goal to inspire all of us to believe ordinary, everyday people can make a difference in their world. But in 2009 the awards inspired those of us from the Philippines for another reason.

That year Filipino Efren Penaflorida became one of nine thousand award nominees selected from one hundred nations. Out of those nine thousand nominees, the panel selected twenty-eight CNN heroes. Efren was among them. Then in October he was named one of the ten finalists. Finally on the twenty-second of November before an audience of three thousand at the Kodak Theater in Hollywood, CNN anchor Anderson Cooper announced that Efren had become the Hero of the Year.

Efren's hero story began at age sixteen. Together with some friends he started a youth group in his high school. Their aim was to divert students' attention away from drugs, alcohol, and gangs and into community activism. So they pioneered the "pushcart classroom."

Pushcarts are used by poor Filipinos to collect junk and scrap for personal use or to resell. Efren took that practice and gave it a new life. His pushcarts were stocked with school supplies, books, tables, and chairs, and used to re-create schools in places where poor children had no access to proper education. Turning trash dumpsites, cemeteries, and other unconventional locations into classrooms, Efren and his friends would teach street children the basics of reading and writing.

Watching the CNN proceedings, I could not help but notice the man who sat beside Efren that evening. I wondered if that was his father, but he looked a tad young to be his dad. Then as the announcement was made, both men rose and embraced each other as Efren made his way to the stage to receive his award. Standing in front of a gathering of admirers, Efren humbly delivered his speech about heroism.

As I watched the proceedings, something about Efren stood out. His meek and humble demeanor was clothed with an equally endearing sense of confidence that spoke to my spirit. Somehow I knew Efren was a disciple of Christ, though he never mentioned Jesus or anything that would communicate that he was a Christian except for a brief allusion to God. It was not until I returned to Manila that I learned Efren was, in fact, a follower of Christ and happened to be a friend of my sister's.

In time Efren and three other men came to dinner at my home. As it turned out, Efren was not the only hero but was part of a tribe of heroes. As the men with Efren were introduced to us, I recognized one of them as the man who was with Efren at the Kodak Theater. I found out that he was Efren's pastor, Bonn Manalaysay.

That evening Bonn told us the story of how Efren became a follower of Jesus. It turns out he was reached through a seemingly insignificant moment of engagement. Apparently Efren grew up in a dumpsite similar to the one that he now serves.

Efren's story was typical of the poor of the Philippines. His father was a motorized pedicab driver, and his mother was a laundrywoman. Efren went to a public school and was reached when he was twelve during a church outreach on his school campus. Initially the young Efren was distant and somewhat indifferent because he had been a victim of much bullying in the past. Bonn recalled that conversations with him were difficult because he usually gave only one-word replies to questions.

Bonn said it was through a gradual process of visiting Efren's home and building a friendship with him over months that Efren began to open up. Bonn also explained that he had to be careful not to come across as a bearer of handouts, which can rob the poor of their dignity. He made sure that when he shared food, it was purely out of a friendship. One year later Efren gave his life to the Lord. And as they say, the rest is history.

What is fascinating to me is how Bonn has managed to raise other disciple makers like Efren and train them all in the same process of engaging people. Imagine the vast difference between Efren the kid in the slums and Efren the Hero of the Year. This is the power of discipleship through relationships. Here again are Stetzer and Putnam on what it means to engage people:

> When we develop churches that speak the language of their community and at the same time hold true to the changeless truth of the Scripture and the gospel, we become successful at breaking the code. Our churches become truly indigenous to their context, and the gospel is able to flow unhindered by cultural barriers.[6]

SOMETHING VERY INTERESTING

Just as in the story of Efren, there is something very interesting that we have seen time and time again when disciples are developed. Social and community outreach increases exponentially without church leadership initiating it.

As a church movement we have an ongoing benevolence initiative known as the Real Life Foundation. Here members of the church serve in feeding programs to young underprivileged children and help provide scholarships and life coaching to high school and university students.

As amazing as Real Life and the work it does are, the church is involved in far more community outreaches. That's because hundreds of disciples have started their own socio-civic activities. Some serve at parachurch ministries such as Habitat for Humanity, the Red Cross, World Vision, Operation Blessing, and Flying Samaritans.

Others take on more organic initiatives. There are doctors and nurses who serve their local communities and small groups that adopt benevolence projects targeting certain neighborhoods. Still others operate full-blown orphanages, and there are those who simply help and serve their marginalized relatives and friends.

These are not programs that need to be headed by full-time staff. They aren't official initiatives, and the leaders don't conduct membership drives in the church. These are simply part of the natural life of the church. The result is hundreds of people are engaged, and many of them become followers of Christ over time. As the people of God embrace His heart for people—His values—they begin moving and acting differently. But let me get back to my point about the principle of engaging one's community and culture.

By now you must be thinking, "When and where is the gospel presented in this model of engaging people in relationships?" Actually it is gradually being presented each time you engage people. Remember that your words, actions, and spirit are communicating. You'll know when the time is right to make a more formal presentation of the gospel. When you have effectively engaged a person, it is just a matter of time before the Holy Spirit prompts you to share the gospel.

To be clear, the goal of engaging people is to present the gospel. This is why even more than learning techniques, formats, and models, we must truly understand the gospel. This is what makes the second section of this book so important. The true power in presenting the gospel lies not merely in knowing how and when to present it, but in making it such a vital and valuable part of our lives that we are compelled to share it with those around us.

There's no doubt that teaching believers when and how to present the gospel is important, as we will discuss later. However, it is our deep appreciation of the truth of the gospel that will make us unable to do anything but share it. When you know what you have is invaluable and inexhaustible, you will gladly give it away.

MORE LIKE A JOURNEY

There are many good books, websites, and materials available that can help you present the gospel effectively. A quick search on Google will give you a long list of resources. It's important that you find a technique that suits your personality and style as well as the people you are reaching.

I default to using Steve Murell's *One2One* soul-winning and discipleship booklet[7] because it is designed to help a person grow gradually in their understanding of who God is and what salvation means. It takes people on a journey into a relationship with God, and when people finally come to accept Christ, they build that relationship on a strong foundation.

In his book *The World at Your Doorstep* Lawson Lau explains that the vast majority of people become followers of Christ over a period of time and not in one "altar-call moment."

> The concept of a spiritual journey suggests that conversion is often a gradual process. In a study of the decision processes of theological students, psychologist Geoffrey Scobie found gradual conversion to be the most common phenomenon.
>
> He says, "The process of growth of belief extends over a period of time, days, months, or even years. During the period the person moves from a position where he is rejecting Christianity as a whole, or some specific part of it, to a point where this rejection has changed to acceptance."[8]

For some the idea of leading people on the journey to salvation seems to miss the urgency of our need to be in a right relationship with Jesus. I believe evangelizing and presenting the gospel is an urgent business that needs serious attention. However, it can be a grave mistake to abruptly present the gospel without considering the person's state of needs or gauging how receptive he may be to the message.

The fact is many of those who are saved at crusades, who seemed to have had a sudden encounter with God on the spot, had many encounters with God's Word and tasted His love from relatives and friends who brought them to the meeting long before they heard the gospel presentation at that event. Some have been sitting in church and have heard the message but only at that moment felt they truly understood who Jesus is and what He did for them. Others have finally counted the cost and weighed its value and decided it was the right decision to make.

Presenting the gospel is, in fact, very urgent business. We need to engage as many people as possible to share with them the good news of Jesus Christ. The only way to present the gospel to more people is for more Christians to engage more people. The more we engage our culture and community, the more opportunities open up to us. Mark Dever explains how biblical evangelism works:

> In biblical evangelism, we don't impose anything. In fact, we really can't. According to the Bible, evangelism is simply telling the good news. It's not making sure that the other person responds to it correctly. I wish we could, but according to the Bible, this is not something we can do. According to the Bible, the fruit from evangelism comes from God....
>
> True biblical, Christian evangelism by its very nature involves no coercion but only proclamation and love. We are to present the free gospel to all; we cannot manipulate anyone to accept it. Biblical Christians know that we can't coerce anyone into life.[9]

GOING THE EXTRA MILE IN PHOENIX

Here is a final story about what it means to engage your community and culture. A few years ago I was teaching on discipleship in Phoenix, Arizona. In the class was a young married couple.

That same afternoon while the couple was taking their dog for a walk, a car pulled up beside them. The driver was lost and asked for directions. He handed them a piece of paper with the address he was looking for. As they read the address, it became apparent that they did not know where it was. The wife walked back to the house with the dog while her husband stood and tried to figure out where the place was. Unable to help, he handed the paper back to the stranger.

As the driver's window went up, he remembered my words that morning: "You don't have to go places. Just make yourself available as you meet people. This is what it means to engage people." So he knocked on the man's window and asked for the note back. While trying to help, he also tried to engage the man in a conversation in hopes of making a connection.

A few more minutes went by, and he still could not figure out the location. The man started getting impatient and wanted his paper back. Just as the stranger was driving away, the man's wife came out of the house with directions to the location mapped out. Apparently she had remembered the lesson that morning sooner than her husband. Women are generally more sensitive than men. She hurriedly searched the Internet and got the directions the driver needed.

Now with the map in hand, her husband flagged the driver down. When the car stopped, he handed the map to the man. The driver was speechless when he learned of the wife's gesture. Deeply moved by their kindness, he quietly replied: "I am an Iranian. I have been in the United States for more than four months, and no one has done anything like this for me." The man gave him his card, and the connection began.

Several weeks later the man invited this couple over for a Persian dinner. There they met his wife, daughters, and another Iranian family. During my last visit to Phoenix they told me that though the man and his family have not come to church, the communication lines remain open and the friendship continues. They had engaged their community and culture and are praying for both families.

I chose to tell this particular story instead of one with a consummated ending because I wanted to show that sometimes engaging does not end with a salvation encounter. We may not be the ones given the privilege of leading the person in the "sinner's prayer." Bill Hybels points out that some of us will simply be part of a person's journey into a relationship with God.

> I believe many people begin their spiritual quest at a negative ten and that my role is to facilitate their movement to a negative eight. That's it. Two points on the spectrum and a result that is still in negative territory. It used to discourage me, but at some point I began to accept the fact that the role I am supposed to play is…well, the role I'm supposed to play.
>
> Likewise, the Spirit might prompt you to take someone who is standing at negative ten a few ticks forward to a whopping negative four. Or you might have the privilege of taking someone who is teetering right on the edge all the way to a positive one, right across the supernatural line of faith. The thrill of it all exists in the fact that as we walk into a spiritual exchange, you and I have no idea what role the Spirit has ordained for us to play.[11]

Sometimes God will give us the opportunity to lead people to that moment of putting their trust in Jesus. It could very well be that someone else sowed the seed, another watered it, and you just happened to be the one who harvested. It is as Jesus said: "Thus the saying 'One sows and another reaps' is true. I sent you to reap what you have not worked for. Others have done the hard work, and you have reaped the benefits of their labor."[12]

At other times we will sow the initial seeds, water seed someone else sowed, or just take the person one step closer to Jesus. In the end only God can make things grow, as Paul said: "I planted the seed, Apollos watered it, but God made it grow. So neither he who plants nor he who waters is anything, but only God, who makes things grow."[13]

By 1968, nineteen years after the first LEGO brick was made, the LEGO company had built a stable and successful play system for children. The company was so successful it built the very first LEGOLAND that year—an entire city of LEGO structures in Billund, Denmark. Something, however, was missing: people.

In 1974 LEGO began making people, starting with the LEGO family. These figures were soon the biggest-selling product that both boys and girls enjoyed. "By 1998, 2.3 billion of these mini figures had been made."[14] LEGO realized that people love people. What good is a world without people?

To the degree that we value and love people will we engage our community and culture. Mark Driscoll put it this way: "If the early church had the same attitude that our church had, the gospel would not have spread and we would have never heard about Jesus. I made it clear that limiting the size of the church for our convenience is a sin and that we should be a church that always exists more for the people who are not yet saved than for the people who are."[15] Amen.

11.

JESUS IS MOST VALUABLE

O UR YOUNGEST SON, Joshua, is affable. He is very positive and knows how to enjoy life. That's why on August 8, 2005, I could tell from his voice that something was wrong.

It was my day off, and Marie and I were watching a movie when my phone vibrated. I walked out of the theater to take Joshua's call. He said, "Pop, Joseph had a bad fall, and we're on our way to the hospital." I asked, "Is it serious?" He tried his best to sound positive, but there was no way around it. "Pop, I think it's serious."

Marie and I arrived at the emergency room at around 7:30 p.m. Joseph, our oldest (then age twenty-two), lay on a gurney with Joshua (age nineteen) standing beside him, still trying his best to stay positive.

Without going into a long explanation, my sons and their friends devised a game on the basketball court. The idea was to do all kinds of acrobatic antics to best one another, including jumping from a platform with a basketball. Did I mention it was raining that day?

Joseph, who is our resident daredevil, fell from thirteen feet headfirst on the concrete floor. Joshua described the fall saying, "It sounded like a bowling ball fell on the ground."

He had multiple fractures in his skull and was internally hemorrhaging fast. In the emergency room Marie calmly cradled the head of her oldest baby as he moaned, "Mom, it really hurts." Joseph was never one to complain. He always had a strong threshold for pain. We knew it was bad. He was delirious and began throwing up blood. Our world was shaking, but that was just the beginning.

It was almost 9:00 p.m. when the doctors finished running tests to determine the right course of action. The neurosurgeon met with Joshua and me and updated us on the situation. He said, "We have to move. We have a sixty-forty percent chance of losing him."

My heart sank. I could feel my knees wobble. Years of raising Joseph flashed through my mind. But it was not time to be emotional. Joseph needed brain surgery fast. And I needed to make a decision.

Deep in my heart I said, "Lord, I really need You now. Don't know if I'll make it. Please help us." I told the doctor, "Let's go ahead and operate."

Huddled in a tiny waiting room, my family sat together. My wife, two sons, sister, and brother-in-law began to pray as we waited for the outcome. Nothing else mattered but the young man in that operating room. In the last few hours what was most valuable to me had become my son's life.

While Joseph was in surgery, more than fifty church members had arrived. They stationed themselves outside the Medical City Hospital, also prayerfully waiting. Their mere presence brought strength and encouragement to our family.

Text messages were sent out and circled the globe. Friends from North America, Europe, Asia, Latin America, Africa, New Zealand, and Australia were mobilized to pray. I can't imagine what that long night would have been like without the comfort and prayers of spiritual family standing with us. This was the body of Christ in action, bringing us comfort when we needed it most.

A PERSONAL FAITH

It had been two hours since they wheeled Joseph into the operating room. My energy was sapped. I knew I had nothing left to hold my family together. I told my middle son, David, to watch over Marie and Joshua while I took some time to pray alone. There is power in praying together and a level of encouragement that comes from our relationship with other believers, but there are times when you just need to be alone with God.

I found a bridge that connected the two buildings of the hospital. It was isolated, and I could see the sky from there. I always liked praying while looking up to the heavens. I said, "God, please don't allow my son to die. I don't know if Marie can take it. I don't know if my faith can handle it. I am afraid, Lord; please help me."

While Christianity is about community, there's also a place where all that's left is our own walk with God. This was one of those places. My wife, children, and I would each grapple with our individual faith.

I am reminded of a time when I told my sons, "When you are young, we take you to church with us. Mom and I will be glad to drive you to your church youth activities. But there will come a time when you can't stand on our faith. You will have to stand on your own." That evening that time had come for all of us.

As I prayed, I was reminded of the night the Lord Himself faced a time of trial. Here was the account of Mark:

> He took Peter, James and John along with him, and he began to be deeply distressed and troubled. "My soul is overwhelmed with sorrow to the point of death," he said to them. "Stay here and keep watch."[1]

Distressed and troubled, Jesus essentially said, "I am overwhelmed to the point of dying." Thankfully, unlike Jesus, I had people who stayed with me and kept watch and prayed. But like Jesus I had to go a little farther to face my own distress alone.

> Going a little farther, he fell to the ground and prayed that if possible the hour might pass from him. "Abba, Father," he said, "everything is possible for you. Take this cup from me. Yet not what I will, but what you will."[2]

In prayer I asked God, "Please don't let this happen to us, but if You should choose to do so, please make me understand that it's not my will but Yours that must prevail. Give me the grace to accept it."

I was also reminded of Abraham when God commanded him to sacrifice his son Isaac. This would test the mettle of my foundations and determine whether they were built right. Reluctantly and with tears in my eyes I said, "Yes, Lord, You can have him. You are my treasure and my great reward."

This was my way of saying, "Lord, You are the 'One True Value' in my life. Please help me!"

It was nearly three in the morning when Joseph, head swathed in bandages covering thirty-nine staples, was wheeled to his room in the intensive care unit. People who have brain surgery are given a set of tests immediately after surgery just to ensure they have not entered a vegetative state or coma. They also checked his memory and thinking process the same morning.

The doctors were methodical in their protocol. In addition to a series of physical examinations and checking his vital statistics, the doctors asked Joseph to count from one to twenty and backward. He was also made to say the alphabet forward and backward. They had him move his fingers, wiggle his toes, and perform other similar tasks. Joseph passed all the tests. We were hopeful.

His surgeon then explained to us the procedure he had just undergone. He said that he had to insert a metal plate to hold Joseph's skull together. Quick as a whip, Joseph cracked a joke. "Does that mean I get a better signal from my cell phone? And what happens when I go through airport security?"

He was back to his usual self. We knew he would be OK. Thank God for His mercy. Like Abraham, figuratively speaking, I did receive Joseph back from death.[3]

Those hours in the hospital with Joseph have been seared in my memory. I am thankful for the grace of God that sustains us in our weakness. More importantly I thank Him for the foundation of Jesus Christ that He has established in each of our lives.

Through the years in our church we've celebrated with people during their high points and wept with them through tragedies. We've seen miraculous healing and bitter disappointment. We saw people give up on their faith during the hard times. But we also saw those who responded in glorious worship and have become a beacon of faith to many more both in the good times and the bad.

The big difference between these two groups of people is that somewhere along the way someone laid the solid foundation of Christ in their lives.

FOUNDATIONS FIRST

In the Gospel of Matthew Jesus explains the importance of laying a solid foundation.

> The rain came down, the streams rose, and the winds blew and
> beat against that house; yet it did not fall, because it had its foun-
> dation on the rock.[4]

In this one verse Jesus explains a simple fact of life: there will be storms
and disasters in life—big, small, personal, local, national, and global. Our
foundations are critical because without them we run the risk of being
overwhelmed by the storms that come our way. In addition to discipleship being about engaging people in relationships, it is also about having
the right foundations in our lives and establishing them in the lives of
others. In the Book of First Timothy we find Paul instructing Timothy
to command believers not to put their hope in the values of this world,
which is so uncertain.

> Command those who are rich in this present world not to be
> arrogant *nor to put their hope in wealth, which is so uncertain,*
> but to put their hope in God, who richly provides us with every-
> thing for our enjoyment.[5]

Instead Paul says they must "put their hope in God." In doing so they
will "lay up treasure for themselves as a *firm foundation* for the coming
age, so that they may take hold of the life that is truly life."[6] This brings
us to the second principle of discipleship.

PRINCIPLE 2: ESTABLISH BELIEVERS IN THE FOUNDATION OF CHRIST

Rice Broocks, cofounder of Every Nation Churches and Ministries, a network of churches that spans the world, wrote about the importance of
spiritual foundations: "We must dig down deep and tear out everything
that is hostile to Christ. We must hear his words—particularly those that
deal with the very foundations of faith—and obey."[7]

Rice is right. Discipleship involves establishing biblical foundations
in the lives of new disciples. The starting point for understanding these
foundations is realizing our foundation is not a religion, belief system, or
church but a person. Jesus is the foundation for all spiritual foundations.

The apostle Paul expressed this truth this way: "For no one can lay any *foundation* other than the one already laid, which is Jesus Christ."[8]

Simply put, the foundation has already been laid; thus we cannot lay it again. Neither can we add to it, enhance it, or, worse, lay a new one. Jesus's one act of dying on the cross and paying the penalty for our sins is the ultimate foundation in our life. There is nothing to add or do but put our faith on His finished work on the cross. It is 100 percent Christ's work and none of ours.

Ultimately He is the One who is most valuable. Without Him there is nothing to build our foundations on. He is the chief cornerstone.[9] In the words of the old hymn, "On Christ the solid rock I stand. All other ground is sinking sand."

When we understand that our foundation is built on nothing but Christ, we realize that we have nothing to offer because He alone gives us life. And since Jesus is 100 percent of our foundation, we are zero. When we come to grips with this truth, we can respond by giving Him 100 percent of our lives, because He alone is worthy of all of it.

Hebrews 6 details for us the "elementary," or foundational, teachings about Christ. These foundational truths represent how we will respond to God when we know that Christ is our one and only foundation:

> Therefore let us leave the elementary teachings about Christ and go on to maturity, not laying again *the foundation* of *repentance* from acts that lead to death, and of *faith* in God, instruction about *baptisms*, the *laying on of hands*, the *resurrection of the dead*, and *eternal judgment*.[10]

These verses in the Book of Hebrews were written to early Christians whose faith was being challenged because they did not understand the elementary teachings about Christ. When we fail to establish these foundational truths, new disciples will be tossed and blown by every wind of teaching.

The writer of Hebrews spells out six foundational responses we will have as we encounter the truth of Jesus Christ: repentance, faith, baptism, the laying on of hands, the resurrection, and judgment. Let's take a quick look at each of these elementary teachings:

Repentance: turning to Christ

Growing up I was raised with an understanding of who Jesus is. However, while I was also lectured on my sinful nature, I was never taught what it meant to repent. Consequently I didn't have that life-giving relationship with God, and my lifestyle showed it. When the gospel became clear to me, I repented of my sins and turned to Christ for salvation. Only then did my life progressively change.

I also realized that repentance is not a one-time event; it has become a continuous part of my life as a Christian. You can call it a "lifestyle of repentance." As Jesus declared, "From that time on Jesus began to preach, 'Repent, for the kingdom of heaven is near.'"[11]

Repentance is not merely turning away from sin. It is turning away from sin because we have turned to Jesus. It is about hating sin so much because we have come to love Jesus so much more we don't want anything to separate us from Him. True repentance is rooted in relationship. How does this happen?

When we come to know Jesus, when He is revealed to us by the Holy Spirit, we realize how much more valuable He is than even our most treasured sin. Not only does the Holy Spirit reveal it to us, but He also gives us the power to resist sin and turn to Him.

Without this foundational truth we end up with flippant Christianity that does not have a firm foundation. Simply put, anyone who continues to willfully live in a sinful pattern has never had the foundation of turning to Christ laid in his life.

Faith: trusting in Christ

When we decide to follow Jesus, what we have is a seed of faith. We must trust Him with our lives and allow that seed to grow. If repentance sets us on the right course, faith causes us to believe God has the power to change us and bring to pass His desired destiny for our lives.

Romans 10:17 tell us that faith comes from hearing from the word of Christ. As we continually hear the message, God's Word comes alive in us and produces this life-changing faith. As we hear and read His Word, He gives us the faith to believe that in Christ: our sins are forgiven,[12] we have been restored into fellowship with the Father,[13] the Holy Spirit has been deposited in us,[14] we can do everything as He strengthens us,[15] all our needs will be met,[16] we are more than conquerors,[17] we have been redeemed from curses,[18] we have confidence to enter the most holy place,[19] we will receive the free gift of eternal life,[20] we are blessed with every spiritual blessing,[21] we have been made righteous,[22] we will have the peace of God that will guard our hearts and our minds,[23] we are seated with Him in heavenly realms,[24] and nothing can separate us from the love of God.[25]

For disciples to overcome the world, we establish them in the foundation of faith in Christ.[26]

Baptism: uniting with Christ

Baptism is about being immersed and soaked in the life of Christ. It also means to be buried with Him in His death.[27] In short, it is to be united with Him in all things. Baptism is also a public declaration of one's allegiance to Christ.

Early Christians stepped out from among the crowds as they responded to the gospel invitation. They allowed themselves to be publicly baptized as a declaration of their union with Christ.[28] It was a declaration that said, "In life and in death I am uniting with You."

A few months after I had given my life to Christ, I was water baptized. That day as I went under the waters of baptism, I publicly declared that my entire life was to be soaked in all that was of Christ. The same waters also symbolized the burial of my old self and the newness of the life I had in Christ as I arose from the water.[29] More than just being a ritual, the act has become a significant pillar in my relationship with Jesus to this day. I am united with Christ in His death and resurrection. Thus I am dead to sin but alive in Christ. This is foundational.

Laying on of hands: working with Christ

Of the six foundational teachings about Christ, the laying on of hands is probably the one that is least explained; as such it is also the least understood. The Bible speaks of different instances of the laying on of hands. Jesus laid hands on people to minister compassion.[30] The laying on of hands is done also as an act of faith to heal the sick,[31] to baptize people in the Holy Spirit,[32] and to impart a gift or a blessing.[33] Done in faith, the laying on of hands is an act that causes Christ's miracles to be seen in people's lives.[34]

We were designed to work with Christ as His fellow workers.[35] Not only did He save us, but He also called us to be used to bring His message to others. Without this foundation we will not experience the fullness of joy that comes from doing the works of Christ.[36]

The laying on of hands means to do the work of ministry with the Lord. It is a foundational truth that Christianity is not merely for our personal benefit and consumption but for us to become vessels of God's Spirit who minister to others.

Resurrection: rising in Christ

Jesus said that He was the resurrection and the life—anyone who believes in Him will live even though he dies.[37] Paul later said, "I have the same hope in God as these men, that there will be a resurrection of both the righteous and the wicked."[38] Furthermore he said that because of this truth, "so I strive always to keep my conscience clear before God and man."[39]

Our understanding of the resurrection life has direct implications on how we conduct our lives on earth. It is also the divine security that assures us of our ultimate destiny. We will resurrect with an imperishable body that is raised in honor, glory, and power; a spiritual body that can go anywhere and do just about anything.[40] Realizing this truth is foundational and of great encouragement to those of us who believe. As the Scriptures declare, "Even in death the righteous have a refuge."[41]

Eternal judgment: glory in Christ

Along with determining whether we will spend eternity in heaven or in hell, the judgment seat of Christ is also where we will receive rewards in the form of crowns in which we will glory in the presence of the Lord Jesus Christ:[42] the victor's crown,[43] the crown of righteousness,[44] the crown of glory,[45] the crown of life.[46]

The whole purpose of these crowns is not so we can parade all over heaven showing them off. These crowns are our way of sharing in the glory of our King. Revelation gives us a picture of that moment in heaven:

> They lay their crowns before the throne and say: "You are worthy, our Lord and God, to receive glory and honor and power, for you

created all things, and by your will they were created and have their being."[47]

What a moment that will be when we stand before our God, laying all our crowns at His feet and giving Him all the glory He deserves, acknowledging that He alone is our reward.[48] This is the fulfillment of the words of Reginald Heber's 1826 classic hymn where it sings: "Casting down their golden crowns around the glassy sea."[49]

Christ—the Living Word

If we are to see people become true disciples of Jesus, we must establish them in biblical foundations. And as we see above, all of these foundations are just facets of the same thing: a relationship with Jesus Christ. The most practical way we can establish these foundations in the people we disciple is to teach them to read and understand the Bible. As Jesus is called the Living Word, this is where we see and know Him best.[50]

The teaching, reading, and study of the Bible are essential in establishing spiritual foundations in the lives of young disciples. In his book *The New Reformation* Greg Ogden writes, "Along with Jesus Christ as both our foundation and the builder on it, the written Word of God is fundamentally connected to establishing and laying foundations in a believer's life."[51]

As disciple makers we must also realize that there will be many lessons we cannot teach people, those that can be learned only from experiencing God Himself through His Word. That's why we need to ensure that the individuals we disciple are established in their relationship with the Lord through His Word.

How we establish these foundations will all vary, just as there are many ways to engage our community and culture. Establishing foundations can be done in classes, one-on-one encounters, through the Internet, via letters, or any other form that works to communicate with those we disciple. However we do it, the goal is to lay foundations. Without these biblical foundations we end up producing syncretistic individuals who tack Jesus on to their amalgamation of different beliefs.

Paul in his first letter to Timothy tells him what must be done in case his arrival is delayed. In this letter Paul explains yet another pillar in the foundation of Christ:

> Although I hope to come to you soon, I am writing you these instructions so that, if I am delayed, you will know how people ought to conduct themselves in God's household, which is *the church* of the living God, *the pillar and foundation* of the truth.[52]

Christ's body, the church, is a vital part of a disciple's foundation. Every disciple must be established in a spiritual community in order to experience lasting growth. As I have recounted earlier, I cannot imagine how my family and I could have endured the very trying ordeal of my son's accident if the church had not supported us in prayer that evening. In recent times there have been pronouncements like, "Jesus I love but not the church." I understand where some of these come from given much of the failures of institutional Christianity that I have mentioned earlier. But this is a very limited view of the body of Christ, His church. There's more to the church than just a religious institution.

While I can take these next pages to give a theological dissertation on the purpose for the church's existence and why we need to establish people in it, I have opted to take a very different tack, a relational one.

More than just joining a sect or denomination, or affiliating with a religious order, being established in the church is about becoming a part of a spiritual family. Take note that in his letter to Timothy, Paul used the words "God's household" to refer to the church. The church is a spiritual community.

It is true that the church has often dropped the ball and has been guilty of many faux pas, but she remains the "body of Christ,"[53] God's ordained vehicle to be His hands and feet in the world and the source of His manifold wisdom on the earth.[54] Jesus is confident the church will triumph and that the gates of hell will not prevail against it.[55]

THE NEW COMMUNITY

Many years ago I did a study of the word *community*. I found that of the eighty-six times the word *community* is used in the Bible, eighty-five of those references were in the Old Testament. Only once was it used in the

New Testament, and in the one New Testament verse where it was used, the word was in reference to the Jewish community.[56]

I am convinced the reason the word *community* practically disappeared in the New Testament was because it had been replaced by another word, *church*. When we study the word *church* in the New Testament, we will find more than one hundred references to it. We can therefore conclude that as far as the Bible is concerned, the new community is the church.

The word *community* first showed up in the Book of Genesis in reference to the descendants of Abraham.[57] The passage infers that the *community* the word refers to is an amalgamation of families who formed into tribes that became the nation of Israel. Similarly churches are composed of families that form local congregations to become the church, or body of Christ, God's family on earth.

No doubt the church has had a long history of fragmentation, splits, and division that dates back to its early days[58] and stretches up to this present day. What family has not had its issues and disputes? But as Jesus prayed, I am confident that when armed with the right set of values, we will all grow, mature, and become one.[59] When we return to the real essence of community, the church will flourish and prosper.

THE FOUNDATION OF JESUS CHRIST

With the gamut of church denominations and fellowship "spin-offs" and the variety of choices in worship styles, how does one know which church is the true church? According to the late Anglican minister David Watson, the primary mark of the church of Jesus is that it will "believe, guard, live by and proclaim the gospel of Christ. Without this, there is no salvation, no knowledge of God and no church."[60] Watson further explains:

> Certainly there are many other elements and factors that constitute church, but the only absolute requirement is to hold fast and to proclaim the gospel of Jesus Christ as revealed in the written word of God, the Scriptures.[61]

Bryan Chapell explains this most basic truth in *Christ-Centered Preaching*:

However, well-intended and biblically rooted a sermon's instruction may be, if the message does not incorporate the motivation and enablement inherent in proper apprehension of the redeeming work of Jesus Christ, the preacher proclaims mere Pharisaism. Preaching that is faithful to the whole of Scripture not only establishes God's requirements but also highlights the redemptive truth that makes holiness possible.[62]

You will know the true church when it upholds, teaches, and preaches that the fullness of life rests on the one foundation of Jesus Christ. He is the One True Value of our lives! As Paul wrote, "See to it that no one takes you captive through hollow and deceptive philosophy, which depends on human tradition and the basic principles of this world rather than on Christ. For in Christ all the fullness of the Deity lives in bodily form, and you have been given fullness in Christ, who is the head over every power and authority."[63]

The first version of the LEGO brick was invented in 1949.[64] Yet as great an invention as the brick was, it was of limited value. Four years later in 1953 things started to change when the company invented the very first LEGO mat, which was then referred to as the "base for building."[65] Without the appropriate foundations LEGO bricks could not build anything worth building.

By 1955, armed with the mat, the company launched the very first "LEGO System of Play: the Town Plan Line."[66] From that point on LEGO bricks could build just about anything.

In a similar way discipleship relationships need strong foundations in order to build disciples for Christ. As Dietrich Bonhoeffer put it, "The life of discipleship can only be maintained so long as nothing is allowed to come between Christ and ourselves. Only by following Christ alone can he preserve a single eye. His eye rests wholly on the light that comes from Christ, and has no darkness or ambiguity in it."[67]

With Jesus as our foundation, there is no limit to the kind of families, churches, and nations that can be built.

12.

MINISTRY IS VALUABLE

MY FATHER WAS a banker. Most of his professional life was spent in the world of valuables: assets, liabilities, collaterals, and cash. Like all of us he was a sinner, but when he was in his mid-fifties, he became a Christian. The result was a clear change in his values. He passionately sought the Lord and freely shared the truth of Christ with his friends and family. Watching him, I learned an incredible lesson about what is of greatest value. In addition to valuing his relationship with Jesus above any material thing, my father showed me the unmatched value of ministry.

It was not unusual to see him share the love of Christ in the course of his day, often in very casual ways. He lived the missional life as a businessman and disciple of Christ. More than just being a follower of Christ, my father helped many become followers themselves.

A few years ago he had to undergo heart bypass surgery. The night before the operation I was at his bedside as the doctors explained to him and the rest of us in the family what the procedure would entail. After the doctors left, my mother, wife, and I prayed for Pop, then he turned to me and asked, "Do you have a *One2One* booklet with you?" I didn't have one of Steve Murrell's discipleship books on me, and I was curious to know why he wanted one at a time like this.

He said, "I've been sharing with the nurse, and I think she wants to know more about Jesus." I shouldn't have been surprised. Such was my father's passion for ministry. I grinned at him and told him to rest up for surgery. I was sure God had the woman covered for now.

As I write this chapter, my father has just turned eighty-two. A week before his birthday I took him and my mother out for dinner. I had some sad news for him, as I was told that one of his close friends was languishing in the hospital fighting cancer. He asked if I was willing to drive him to visit his friend.

It was a Monday morning when my father and I visited the hospital. His friend was struggling to breathe and was unable to speak. He could communicate only with groans and gestures. Both men were eighty-one years old and have been friends for almost sixty years. The lone caregiver placed a chair beside the bed where my father sat and proceeded to speak with his friend. I sat on the sofa behind him.

My father began by thanking his friend for their years of friendship. He recalled some of their escapades in their younger days. His friend acknowledged our presence and my father's kind words by gesturing with his hand. A few minutes into the exchange, my dad's friend drifted into a snooze. The caregiver explained that he was struggling to stay conscious and that he had been this way for a while.

Sensing that he had limited time, my father said these words when his friend awoke: "Death could come today, tomorrow, next week, or even next year, but it will come. And there's only one thing to do about it. Only Jesus can transport us to eternity with Him. I have come today to bring you the message of God's love and grace toward you. I know that you have in times past laughed at the words I have shared with you about Jesus, but He is your God and my God, and He is the only one who can save you from your sins. If you acknowledge your need of a Savior, He will save you right here and now. Would you like to do that?"

By now the caretaker had tears flowing. She was witnessing a human drama as one friend expressed his love and concern for another. My dad's friend responded with a groan that was hard to translate. We are not certain if his response was a yes. Then he drifted back to sleep.

After some more exchanges with the caretaker it was time to leave. As I helped my father out of his chair, his friend awoke again. His eyes open but still unable to speak, he extended his hand to my father. They shook hands and then he reached toward me, wanting to shake my hand as well. As I took his hand, it felt like an old friend was saying thank you and good-bye. I prayed for my dad's friend, that God would grant him peace and comfort but more importantly that he would trust in His grace and mercy. Then we bade him good-bye.

As I escorted my father out of the room, I could sense a kind of joy in his weak step; his countenance beamed with confidence that he had done God's will. In the elevator I told him, "You did good today, Pop." He looked at me and smiled.

In the car I pondered the whole experience. Would this dying man have had a chance of hearing the gospel if my father did not value ministering to him? The other question was, how many Christians would be willing to go and do what he did but don't have the confidence because they don't feel competent to minister? Then I wondered how many situations like this one happen in the course of a day as Christians stand helplessly by because they were not equipped to minister.

Those questions still roll around in my head, which brings us to the third principle of discipleship.

PRINCIPLE 3: EQUIP ALL BELIEVERS TO MINISTER

A common practice that has hampered the church when making disciples is that after we have engaged people and established them in spiritual foundations, we fail to equip them to become effective ministers. The late Harvard and Stanford universities chaplain Elton Trueblood captured the essence of this flagrant failure:

> Perhaps the greatest single weakness of the contemporary Christian Church is that millions of supposed members are not really involved at all and, what is worse, do not think it strange that they are not.[1]

This has stripped the kingdom of God of workers and harvesters that it so greatly needs and is the very lifeblood of ministry. To this Trueblood said:

> There is no real chance of victory in a campaign if ninety percent of the soldiers are untrained and uninvolved, but that is exactly where we stand now. Most alleged Christians do not now understand that loyalty to Christ means sharing personally in His ministry, going or staying as the situation requires.[2]

Discipleship means it is not enough to establish believers in the foundation of Christ; we must equip them to become effective ministers. The goal of equipping disciples is to give them the competence and the confidence to do the work of ministry.

Paul Becker, Jim Carpenter, and Mark Williams in their handbook on church planting explain that the Greek word employed for "preparing" or "equipping" was *katartizo*.

> In every case, the "preparing" or "equipping" pictures a transformation from brokenness to wholeness, from ineffectiveness to usefulness. When a torn fishing net was dragged up on the beach and mended so that it could be used again, it was "equipped."[3]

The picture of a torn net that has been rendered ineffective validates the importance of equipping people in ministry. Equipping means mending the net so it can function properly. Interestingly when Jesus called His first disciples into ministry, He found them while they were casting a net into the lake.

"As Jesus was walking beside the Sea of Galilee, he saw two brothers, Simon called Peter and his brother Andrew. They were *casting a net* into the lake, for they were fishermen."[4] Then He said, "Come, follow me...and I will make you fishers of men."[5]

In this one summons Jesus captured the essence of the ministry of discipleship and what disciples need to be equipped in. Discipleship is about following Jesus while being in fellowship with other believers as they fish for people together.

- Follow Jesus

- Fellowship with believers

- Fish for people

Notice that in each facet of ministry is a vital relationship: Jesus, other believers, and people in general. Equipping believers in ministry means tightening their relationship with God and with other believers so they can together reach the world for Jesus—the closer the ties and the tighter the knots, the greater the net's ability to reach people. Steve Addison affirms the value of relationships in discipleship ministry in his book *Movements That Changed the World*: "Like a virus, the gospel travels along lines of preexisting relationships. Christian conversions followed networks of relationships."[6]

Any equipping program focused on discipleship must also train believers to demonstrate commitment, power, and wisdom in each of these three areas. In his book *The Three Colors of Ministry* Christian Schwarz points out how we often find people who are zealous in doing ministry but lack wisdom. Then there are those who have wisdom and commitment but lack the power that comes by faith. Much of ministry is undertaken in the strength of the flesh. Then there are those who have wisdom and power but are not as committed. Even the wisest and most gifted are useless if they are absent.

There are a variety of curricula for equipping believers in ministry, such as Schwarz's. Our own fellowship has a comprehensive curriculum that has worked effectively over the years. However, our experience also shows that while classes help, mentoring relationships are by far the best way to train and equip disciples.

This chapter, however, seeks to emphasize the goal rather than the actual curriculum for equipping disciples.

CASTING AND HAULING THE NET

As I already expressed, the goal of closer ties and stronger knots is not just so we can enjoy our relationships with God and one another. Our strong relationships are to be like a well-mended net that is designed for a reason and a mission to reach others.

When Jesus spoke of fishing, His context was not what we in the modern world understand it to be. Fishing to Jesus was using a net and not a pole. For starters, unlike with pole fishing, a person cannot fish with a net alone. Net fishing requires other hands and a partner (or partners) to cast a net.

We see in the Gospel of Mark that as "Jesus walked beside the Sea of Galilee, he saw Simon and his brother Andrew casting a net into the lake, for they were fishermen."[7] When Jesus called His disciples to fish for people, His intent was that they do it in teams. The context was relational. Fishing is always more enjoyable, effective, and efficient when you do it with others.

The net fishing analogy also illustrates two other important points. First, nets have to be deliberately let down into the sea of humanity and not kept in a beach or a boat.

> When he had finished speaking, he said to Simon, "Put out into deep water, and *let down the nets for a catch*."[8]

Second, net fishing needs partners to haul in the harvest.

> When they had done so, they caught such *a large number of fish* that their nets began to break. So *they signaled their partners* in the other boat *to come and help them*, and they came and filled both boats so full that they began to sink.[9]

Just as with net fishing, we need to be trained and equipped to do the work of ministry in partnership with others. One vital way to accomplish this is through small groups. Not only did Jesus make disciples in small groups, but it is also by far the most practical and effective way to disciple people. A small group is like a net that is connected to other small groups that combine to form a larger net that is cast into the sea of humanity every day.

In their book *Mentor Like Jesus* Regi Campbell and Richard Chancy capture the essence of why Jesus discipled people in small groups:

> That is the critical thing Jesus understood about investing in the disciples. He knew how difficult their path would be after He was gone, and He knew they wouldn't be capable of doing it alone. So he gave them the gift of brotherhood...guys with a common vision and passion. They never went out in the world alone; they were always in groups of at least two. They lived in relationship with one another. And they understood those relationships were crucial to the success of their mission.[10]

Over the years our church has developed training programs on how to make disciples in and through small groups that are based on the values and principles mentioned in this book. The better equipped we become, the better we will be at equipping others in ministry. Imagine what would happen if Christians all over the world were mended into relationships that fully equipped them to do the work of ministry.

THE ROLE OF DISCIPLINE

The topic of equipping disciples in ministry would not be complete without touching on the subject of discipline. Many discipleship programs have a strong emphasis on discipline. Even a child can observe that the words "dis-ci-ple" and "dis-ci-pline" are made up of three syllables that are akin to one another.

One of the first Christian books I read as a believer was Elisabeth Elliot's *Discipline: The Glad Surrender*. It was a gift given to me by a friend when I was but a month old in my faith. In it I found a unique perspective on discipline. According to Elisabeth Elliot, discipline is born of relationship:

> As a child in a Christian home, I did not start out with an understanding of the word discipline. I simply knew that I belonged to the people who loved me and cared for me. That is dependence. They spoke to me and I answered. That is responsibility. They gave me things to do, and I did them. That is obedience. It adds up to discipline.[11]

I thank God that even back then He was teaching me that discipline, and consequently discipleship, is borne in relationship. Here again is Steve Addison: "Spiritual disciplines may vary from movement to movement, but they are all activities that deepen our relationship with God."[12]

At this point I must issue a word of caution. Richard Foster, author of the classic *Celebration of Discipline*, wisely warns of how easily disciplines can be turned into legalism:

> The Spiritual Disciplines are intended for good. They are meant to bring the abundance of God into our lives. It is possible, however, to turn them into another set of soul-killing laws.[13]

And how does one keep this from happening? By understanding that discipline was designed for the purpose of building relationships first with God then with one another.

We must also be clear that discipline does not save us from our sins, for only God's grace saves; salvation cannot be earned by any effort on our part. The role of discipline is to understand the frailty of our human nature; the spirit is willing but the flesh is weak. It was the undisciplined flesh of the disciples that failed to watch and pray. It eventually led them to abandon the Lord.

GROWING IN DISCIPLINE

"God did not give us a spirit of timidity but a spirit of power, of love, and of self-discipline."[14] The goal of training and equipping disciples is to see them grow to one day have a spirit of power, love, and self-discipline. Take note I did not say a spirit of being under discipline or accountability that is administered by another, but to grow in "self-discipline."

It was my friend Paul Barker who shared with me the best way to picture discipline. He said it's like a narrow ledge. We can fall off on either side. On the one side we can become passive believers who have no sense of duty, responsibility, or urgency for the things of God's kingdom. On the other side we can become legalistic strivers who can turn discipline into a law that demands performance.

Discipline is the balancing act that allows us to temper the weakness of our flesh. It causes us to obey because we love God and value what He values while making sure that we do not succumb to legalism and a wrong theology based on man's works and effort. Over time as we are trained in righteousness through our relationship with God, it becomes second nature, or self-discipline.

The goal of equipping believers is to turn believers into self-disciplined disciples in the way they follow Jesus, fellowship with other believers, and fish for people.

We have all heard the stories of successful artists, athletes, and individuals who recount how a parent, grandparent, teacher, coach, or mentor disciplined them to become who they are in their field.

From Yo-Yo Ma to Michael Phelps, people who embrace discipline do not initially enjoy it. However, over time as they have gotten the hang of it and embraced the process of discipline, it became second nature to them. Once equipped with certain disciplines, they started to enjoy themselves in the discipline they have mastered. Picture Andrea Bocelli making music and Manny Pacquiao boxing in the ring—you can tell that amid all the pressure to perform they enjoy what they do.

We often do not enjoy the process of discipline. The funny thing, however, is we all want and admire the fruit of discipline when we see it. This is also true of our faith and discipleship. As new believers we can resent the discipline that is being brought into our life. The process is not always easy and enjoyable, but as we stay in a relationship with God and with other believers, we eventually get the hang of it as these disciplines become a part of our lives. The fruit not only become enjoyable but also invaluable.

John Ortberg points out the value of a disciplined life: "Disciplined people...can do the right thing at the right time in the right way for the right reason."[15]

"WHAT ABOUT MY GIFTS?"

People often ask me, "Where do my spiritual gifts fit into all this equipping?" The answer is in discipleship. Use your spiritual gifts as you go and make disciples. Often I find pastors tend to overemphasize the area of training people in their gifts rather than equipping them in spiritual disciplines and in the ministry of discipleship.

There is obviously a valid place for specialized training for worship leaders, musicians, those with a gift of evangelism or prophecy, and those who serve in other specialized church roles. But the vast majority of people must be trained in the ministry of making disciples, of mending the nets into a relationship with God and others. This is something everyone can do and should do.

I am reminded of a time I was training pastors and leaders in Washington DC. While dining at the Cheesecake Factory with my son David and the two pastors who were hosting us, they asked the question I mentioned previously, "Where do people's gifts fit into all this training?" I told them what I have just told you, that the gifts are used in discipleship.

I noticed that while my point was crystal clear to David, the two pastors struggled to understand it. My son grew up in a church that equipped and empowered people to make disciples. They were steeped in a culture that focused on "my gifts" and "my talents," one that catered to the "super Christian," the performer who needs to express gifts particularly during a church service. The culture they were used to was often about "the man or woman of God" and their gifting, the very thing that disables the rest of the body.

Fortunately God provided the perfect answer to their question, our waitress. She was a tall, attractive woman. I engaged in conversation with her by asking her name and how long she had been working as a waitress. She said, "Oh no, I'm just a temp. I'm an aspiring singer. I just do this part-time and will be moving soon."

"Wow," I said, "that's great. Would you sing for us?" She replied, "I can't do that. I'm on duty." Amazingly she knew the principles of ministry more than some Christians. She understood that her talents and gifting were secondary to her duties. Jesus said, "So you also, when you have done everything you were told to do, should say, 'We are *unworthy servants; we have only done our duty.*'"[16]

As our waitress left, I explained to the two men the reality about gifts. Churches and fellowships should not try to create functions and roles because of people's gifts. Roles should be defined based on the functions needed to make disciples. Our gifts must be utilized for making disciples. I capped my point by asking, "What do you do when you have more singers than you need?"

Members of God's household should realize the role and function of the church does not revolve around their gifts and talents, much like our waitress who understood her job right then was to serve no matter how great her singing gift may be. Our attitude should be if our gifts can be utilized during a worship service, then we gladly serve; if not, we continue to function in the ministry of making disciples.

THE ROLE OF FIVEFOLD MINISTRY

I told the leaders in Washington that sometimes Cheesecake Factory managers are better leaders than pastors. They know what needs to be done as well as what they want done. Then they get people to do it. Then I said, "Our job is not to build on people's gifts but to go and make disciples and get everyone to do whatever it takes to do the same, which includes using their gifts." That night I saw two light bulbs switch on.

At the time both men were leading a church that had a fluctuating membership of about 160 people. Today more than 600 attend the church, and many of them are disciples who make disciples right in downtown DC. More importantly, they have learned how to equip disciples in the work of ministry.

The more discipleship relationships form, the more ministry opportunities there are. Thus people's gifts are fully maximized and not just utilized for Sunday services but in a variety of other settings. Needless to say we should know, appreciate, and maximize our gifts but not allow our gifts to be the preeminent thing that governs everything we do. No matter what our gift is, we should be ready to make disciples.

I also explained to the men that our role as church leaders is not to do the work of ministry. Scripture clearly tells us what the role of leaders and members are: "It was *he who gave some to be apostles*, some to be prophets, some to be evangelists, and some to be pastors and teachers, *to prepare* God's people *for works of service.*"[17]

The role of ministers is to equip or prepare people to do the work of ministry. The work of service or ministry is the function of members. Sadly there are leaders who focus on people's gifts, and there are those who are consumed by their own. They become the lone visionary, the super Christian, the "Anointed One," "the Man of God," or, at worst, a celebrity.

The role of ministers in equipping is for a very clear purpose: "that the body of Christ may be built up until we all reach unity in the faith and in the knowledge of the Son of God and become mature, attaining to the whole measure of the fullness of Christ."[18] As ministers equip and members are trained, we will experience greater unity, faith, maturity, and the whole measure of the fullness of Christ.

At present our church in metro Manila has approximately sixty thousand people who attend ninety-one services in fifteen locations overseen by teams of pastors. While I oversee the church in Metro-Manila, I can walk into one of these services, and most of the people around me have no clue who I am. That's because the person they know is their lead pastor and their small group friends and members. My role is to lead those who minister and make disciples myself.

This translates to hundreds of volunteers who serve in all the ministries that take place every weekend. These include the worship teams, children's and preteens' ministry, administration, ushering, technical support, hospitality, and many others. Prayer, counseling, and even pastoral care are done by disciples and take place in small groups. When faced with challenging cases and situations (mostly involving legal matters), small group leaders are equipped to elevate these concerns to the better trained full-time ministers.

These ministries require thousands of volunteers to perform these functions week in week out, year in year out. In our experience there is no shortage of volunteers for these activities when a congregation is full of trained, equipped, and prepared disciples.

Johan Roos and Bart Victor of Switzerland's IMD School of Business used LEGO as the medium for their training programs. They called the program "LEGO Serious Play."

At the core of LEGO Serious Play is Seymour Papert's theory of constructionism. Papert, an MIT professor, theorized that people learn by building something that helps explain and define relationships. Today companies such as Daimler Chrysler, Roche Pharmaceutical, Tupperware, and Nokia use the program, as do a number of nongovernmental organizations worldwide.

As Christians, we too need to "get out of our box." By that I mean we should keep the essential and eternal truths of Jesus's teachings while challenging the usual way we train and equip others. This way we can stay relevant to the world we live in without watering down the gospel of Christ. We can develop curricula like LEGO Serious Play that contain timeless truths of the Bible while adjusting our presentation to fit the current context and realities of the people we are training. In this way we can build a net that reaches the world with the gospel.

13.

EVERY DAY IS VALUABLE

JAMES CAMERON'S SCI-FI adventure movie *Avatar* has become the biggest box office hit ever. Watching it in IMAX 3D brought the movie's special effects to a whole other level. Though the story line was predictable and to some looked like Pocahontas in outer space, the creativity of the film was a definite "wow" and well worth the 162-minute run time.

The movie was set in the year 2154. Pandora is a lush rainforest planet somewhere in outer space. The plot involved a mining company that was there to extract the precious "unobtanium"—a mineral that could solve earth's growing energy crisis. It was valued at twenty million dollars a kilo back on earth.

The tension in the story began with the discovery that the biggest deposit of the mineral lay underneath the habitation of the peaceful Na'vi, one of Pandora's indigenous inhabitants. After diplomatic efforts fail to move the Na'vi, the greedy boss of the mining company and his hired mercenaries cruelly attack the Na'vi to forcibly eject them.

Caught in the crossfire were a handful of employees who did not agree with the mining company's directives. Thus at the center of the story was a conflict in values. The materialistic humans coveted a lifeless mineral and the wealth that came with it, regardless of the cost, while the Na'vi and their human friends treasured life.

In bringing up the movie, I am not in any way advocating a syncretistic or New Age worldview. My aim is to show that some struggles are universal. Whatever our age, race, social class, or religious upbringing, there is always that tension between good and evil, between a higher cause and a lesser good. Young and old you could hear and feel the viewers cheering for the minorities and the underdogs. Why? Because above it all there is such a thing as "universal values."

THE SIX THINGS WE VALUE

Jesus spoke about man's universal values in Matthew 6. This chapter is where we find Jesus teaching that values are a matter of the heart: "For where your treasure is, there your heart will be also."[1] It was after He spoke these words that He outlined the six universal values of man. He started out by saying:

> No one can serve two masters. Either he will hate the one and love the other, or he will be devoted to the one and despise the other. You cannot serve both *God and Money*.[2]

Jesus used universally valued money in contrast with the God of the universe. The verses that follow outline the rest of what is universally valued or what is most important to people.

> Therefore I tell you, do not worry about your life, what you will eat or drink; or about your body, what you will wear. Is not *life more important than food*, and the *body more important than clothes*?[3]

In these verses Jesus the master teacher is showing us three pairs of contrasts:

- God and money

- Life and food

- Body and clothes

Why these three pairs? It's because in each pair there is one that is *more* valuable than the other. God is infinitely more valuable than money, life more than food, and our bodies more than clothes. Also in this verse Jesus teaches that much of our worrying comes from a faulty hierarchy of what is valuable.

THE HIERARCHY OF VALUES

We have made it clear in previous chapters that God has the ultimate value. That's because He is the standard of all that is valuable. We worship Him because He is worthy (worth it). He deserves our utmost worship because He is most valuable.

Values can only be esteemed when they are measured against a standard. That standard is God. He is the Creator of all life. Failure to appraise based on an appropriate standard will result in a wrong valuation of everything else of value. If a person fails to recognize that God and life are of greatest value, one would probably have a faulty valuation of most everything else.

From these three pairs of values we can distill two sets of values, what I call the higher or "Top Line" values and the lower or "Bottom Line" values:

Top Line	Bottom Line
God	Money
Life	Food
Body	Clothes

Let's discuss the top line values first. Next to God our lives and our bodies are most important. What good is money if we don't have life and a healthy body?

I am reminded of a time a doctor had wrongly diagnosed a sore throat I had and said it could be cancer. My youngest son, Joshua, accompanied me to the doctor, and we were both shocked at his prognosis. That evening and in the days that followed, the last thing I could think of was money, food, or clothes. All of a sudden nothing was more valuable than God, my life, and my body. Fortunately after I sought a second opinion, the first doctor was proven wrong.

When faced with such a threat, the financial markets, our assets, our political predispositions, global warming and the environment, and all other concerns all take a backseat—nothing matters more than God, life, and good health. If you think about it, the reason we are concerned about the environment is because it affects our lives and bodies. As best-selling author Jared Diamond puts it, "I am more interested in environmental issues because of what I see as their consequences for people than because of their consequences for birds."[4]

After God, it boils down to two things: our life and our body. These are the two things that are of utmost value to people universally.

Consider this question: If your house was on fire, what would you grab first on your way out? I have asked more than a hundred people this question, and their initial answers have been as varied as car keys, marriage contract, laptop, jewelry, family pictures, mobile phone, and passport.

But after some reflection, the overwhelming answer people give is that they'd just want to get out alive. Whether it's people trapped at the World Trade Center or the Chilean miners buried under the earth, when push comes to shove, we drop everything and value life and body. After the recent earthquake and tsunami combo in Japan, the rescuers' primary concern was not money, food, or things; in the rubble they were looking for lives and bodies.

PSUCHE AND SOMA

The Gospel writers employed the Greek words *psuche* for life and *soma* for the body. *Psuche* means that which has breath, spirit—in other words, life. Our lives constitute more than just our bodies. Life is about living, moving, and having our being. To have life means to have hope. Why is our life more valuable than all the other things in our home? It's because if our photographs burn in the fire, we can always take new ones. But if our lives perish in the flames, there will be no one to enjoy the pictures. As long as we have life, anything is possible. That's why Solomon said, "Anyone who is among the living has hope—even a live dog is better off than a dead lion!"[5]

Life does not just mean our own personal lives but everything that has breath. *Marley and Me* author John Grogan can only agree with Solomon, that if his house was on fire he would take himself and his family out first and then Marley—everything else can burn up. I would do the same thing, for life also represents the lives of our spouses, children, families, and friends—our relationships, much of what this book is about.

Again Jared Diamond confesses that his underlying concern for the environment is motivated by his love for people, particularly his closest relationships, "But while I do love New Guinea birds, I love much more my sons, my wife, my friends, New Guineans and other people."[6]

Soma meant our physical bodies. To Jesus, this too was of great importance and value. Ravi Zacharias explained the value of the body this way:

> Your body and my body are His temple. There is an extraordinary conferral of sanctity upon what it means to be human. It means that this body is deemed worthy of respect and reverence....
>
> All the desacralizing that has engulfed our culture lies in this very struggle to understand the place and sacredness of the body...all of these flow from the fact that this body becomes the dwelling place of God. Our world would be a different place if we comprehended this sobering privilege.[7]

Often the emphasis of Christians is only on matters of the spirit, mind, will, and emotions. We take for granted that we are embodied creatures. I have found that being spiritual and living life can be challenging when my body is unhealthy. Even the apostle Paul underscored the merit and value of caring for our bodies when he wrote, "For physical training is of some value."[8]

As a parting shot, John the Beloved wrote in his letter a prayer for the physical health of the disciples. Theologians say he could have been in his late eighties or nineties when he said, "Dear friend, I pray that you may enjoy good health and that all may go well with you, even as your soul is getting along well."[9]

Here again we find that our spiritual and natural life overlaps. We can't read our Bibles and go to church without our bodies or live life without our relationships or run a marathon without our spirits. Discipleship is not just a matter of information transfer, but it must have an application in all areas of our life. Our bodies are important.

Meanwhile back in Matthew 6, Jesus's real big point was in the verse that followed the one with the three pairs of contrasts. He said, "Look at the birds of the air; they do not sow or reap or store away in barns, and yet your heavenly Father feeds them. Are you not much more valuable than they?"[10]

We are valuable not merely because of our own intrinsic worth but because God, who is most valuable, values us. In the world around us, value increases depending on the demand for a certain product, commodity, or service. This is true of real estate, stocks, bonds, and even art.

Value also increases because of who desires the instrument, product, or service. Share prices of stocks and bonds go up depending on the governments, investment houses, or even individuals who buy them. Art pieces get sold at ridiculously high prices because a billionaire called the artist "sublime."

The world works this way because that was how God shaped our hearts. It is our inability to valuate correctly that often gets us in trouble.

Chief among our understanding of values is that we are valuable only because God, who is most valuable, values us, and anything that has value has a corresponding cost. The apostle Paul said, "God demonstrates his own love for us in this: While we were still sinners, Christ died for us."[11]

In reality, nothing of value is free. If it is free, then it either has no real value or someone paid the cost so others may enjoy it. Salvation is free and valuable because God paid for our sins. He loves us so much that He "did not spare his own Son, but gave him up for us all."[12] He so valued us that He gave us what was most valuable to Him.

THE VALUE OF EACH DAY

In every recorded interaction that Jesus has with people, we see Him making disciples as He went on His way living His life in His body. He valued each day. He attended weddings, visited with friends, played with children, and was present at funerals. His messages reveal a life that was fully lived out. He talked about agriculture, construction, education, the environment, garments, health, and even wine. He understood the world of finance and wealth, politics and power, religion and culture.

He used this information to engage and teach. The Bible also says He slept, ate, prayed, worked, and went to the synagogue. He lived out life in His body while building relationships and making disciples. He modeled the very idea of going and making disciples every day.

Ed Stetzer and David Putnam explain what it means to "go and make" disciples while living life in our body in their book *Breaking the Missional Code*:

The word *go* in the text is the aorist participle *pareuo* in the Greek and carries with it the idea of "while you go," "in your going," and/or "as you go."[13]

Jesus was empowered to make disciples as He lived His life in His body every day. This is our goal as disciples of Jesus and as disciple makers. After we engage, establish, and equip new disciples, we must empower all believers to make disciples.

PRINCIPLE 4: EMPOWER ALL BELIEVERS TO MAKE DISCIPLES

At the heart of this final discipleship principle is the phrase *as we go*: to work, to school, to play, to visit relatives, to the grocery, to the salon, to soccer matches, to church, to dine with friends, on a business trip, to bowling night, for lunch break, to Pilates class, on Facebook, to a small group meeting, and lay with our children in bed. In short, as we do "life" in our "body" every day, we go and make disciples.

There's more good news. Before Jesus ascended into heaven He gave us a more promise: "Do not leave Jerusalem, but wait for the gift my Father promised, which you have heard me speak about. For John baptized with water, but in a few days you will be baptized with the Holy Spirit."[14]

Then He said in same vein, "But you will receive power when the Holy Spirit comes on you; and you will be my witnesses in Jerusalem, and in all Judea and Samaria, and to the ends of the earth."[15]

More than just being equipped, we are empowered by God to be His witnesses here on earth. Through the Holy Spirit He confirms His relationship with us,[16] He teaches and reminds us His Word,[17] He will tell us what to say,[18] and He helps us in our weakness.[19] God empowers us to live out not just the first three of His universal values but all six.

There's no doubt God, life, and body are far more valuable than money, food, and clothes. Yet we must realize that Jesus never said money, food, and clothes are not valuable. What He said was that God, life, and body—the top-line values—are more important.

Losing our jobs and our incomes has far-reaching effects on our spiritual lives, relationships, and health as well as our witness and testimony to others. The reality is money is not the real problem, greed is. Similarly food and the things we enjoy are God-given; it is gluttony and lust that undermine their value. Finally clothes and material things have obvious values. They are not the problem; materialism is. Materialism is the belief that materials are all that matters.

What does this tell us? As Christians we must live out our faith cognizant of the fact that it has an application not only in the first three values of God, life, and body but also in all of the six universal values. Our Christianity must also encompass money, food, and clothes.

MONEY—"THE ANSWER TO EVERYTHING"

Our earlier discussion on money showed how it can easily become "the god" we look to. However, we all know that life on earth cannot be lived without money. With this is mind the words of Solomon ring true:

> A feast is made for laughter, and wine makes life merry, but money is the answer for everything.[20]

Many people don't even realize that is in the Bible. Before you draw conclusions about these words, let me explain an important principle in reading Scripture. Heresies are often derived when we reason from a part of the Bible and not its whole counsel. In studying and interpreting the Bible, one should never reason from a part of Scripture to the whole but always from the whole to the part.

As a whole the Bible says money can become a god that enslaves people and that those "who want to get rich fall into temptation and a trap and into many foolish and harmful desires that plunge men into ruin and destruction."[21] Furthermore it states, "For the love of money is a root of all kinds of evil. Some people, eager for money, have wandered from the faith and pierced themselves with many griefs."[22]

So what exactly did Solomon mean when he wrote, "Money is the answer for everything"?

Despite the fact that Solomon wrote the Book of Ecclesiastes in a "backslidden" state, the Holy Spirit has allowed the words of this book to bring us vital truths. Solomon was reasoning from the part. He also wrote this verse in the context of how to run a government as a king. He was expressing that while feasts and merriment, food and wine can mitigate the concerns of people, ultimately money or economic solutions are the lasting answer to people's needs. They need and want money over enjoyment.

Solomon's earthly perspective also points out that people love to eat, drink, and celebrate. Next to money people crave for food, drink, and celebrations—all symbolic of merriment and enjoyment. This aligns with Jesus's hierarchy of values, where money is followed by food or things we crave and enjoy.

The obvious reason money is ranked more valuable than food and enjoyment is because it can buy food, drinks, and fun. Money is more valuable because it is capable of purchasing what we crave and a whole lot more. As disciples and disciple makers we need to confront the truth that while God, life, and body are the greater values, economics and enjoyment are important and valuable as well.

Many times Christians are guilty of burying their heads in the sand. They refuse to confront the reality that unless God's Word and our discipleship programs address matters pertaining to economics and enjoyment, they have limited value, especially to unbelievers and new believers. People instinctively know that our lives go beyond the stereotypical brand of Christianity that seems to always talk about spirituality and family.

The Bible has a lot to say about this second set of values, but Christians often dodge the discussion. They come across as clueless, holier-than-thou folks with boring lives. Howard Dayton, CEO of Crown Financial Ministries, correctly observed that:

> Sixteen of the 38 parables were concerned with how to handle money and possessions. Indeed, Jesus Christ said more about money than about almost any other subject. The Bible offers 500 verses on prayer, fewer than 500 verses on faith, but more than 2,350 verses on money and possessions.[23]

Nationally syndicated Christian radio talk-show host and financial adviser Dave Ramsey writes about how money affects our most basic relationships.

> The very core of the family is dramatically affected by this over-buying, which creates overborrowing. Most marriages that fail

list financial problems as a contributing factor, if not the main reason for the failure.[24]

The way we value money and the things we enjoy and buy have serious implications on our most important relationships.

Does that mean we should be driving a Jaguar and wearing the latest fashions in order to speak about wealth and money? Nope. Dave Ramsey repeatedly points out that much of financial success is rooted in hard work, contentment, and the ability to save more than we spend. What it means is that we should know what God has to say about money, live these precepts, and be able to model and teach them to others.

As Franky Schaeffer correctly observed, "The commitment to moral and spiritual values goes hand in hand with a prosperous economy."[25] God has a lot to say about wealth, property, and money. One of Steve Murrell's most popular Bible studies for small groups is titled *How to Manage God's Money*. The material was a hit not just with Christians but also among those who were not believers. They were amazed to know how much God has to say about wealth and money.

If Christians do not disciple people in all six universal values, we will succeed in raising spiritual people who may love God and their families but have no ability to stay healthy, wealthy, and wise. Worse, they may be moral when it comes to God and family but amoral, if not immoral, when it pertains to their work, finances, and the things they enjoy.

ON DISMISSING PROSPERITY

Since I discussed enjoyment in an earlier chapter, let me focus on matters pertaining to prosperity here. Depending on their background, some Christians are quick to dismiss so-called "prosperity preachers." We accuse them of reducing the gospel to promises of "health and wealth." No doubt some leaders have manipulated people with false promises of material wealth and wellness.

But we do not want to be guilty of throwing the baby out with the bathwater. Our overreaction to some who preach this message may cause us to deprive people of the truth about God's ability to bless His people with good health and wealth. When we do, we short-circuit God's ability to transcend the natural and meet His people at their need.

If discipleship is to be real, we must help people believe that the words of the Bible are not empty promises. And to hold to these promises as gospel truth, God desires to meet His children in *all* their needs. As the apostle Paul stated, "And my God will meet *all* your needs according to his glorious riches in Christ Jesus."[26]

Along with all the other things involved in discipleship, it is also about imparting faith that God is *still* in the business of performing miracles. Here theologian GK Chesterton is worth quoting: "The most incredible thing about miracles is that they happen."[27]

Many people have put their faith in Christ not simply because of His teaching but also because of His miracles, as the writer of the Gospel of John notes: "Then the father realized that this was the exact time at which Jesus had said to him, 'Your son will live.' So he and all his household believed."[28]

Christians must take God at His Word and declare that He "is able to do immeasurably more than *all* we ask or imagine, according to his power that is at work within us."[29]

You cannot read the four Gospels without seeing that miracles are a big part of God's work. Discipleship is empowering people to believe that the Holy Spirit is alive and well and desires to move in and through their lives to manifest His power and love as they minister to others.

I have found that the disdain certain quarters have toward "signs and wonders" is not their unwillingness to believe God is no longer in the business of miracles but in the way it is taught and how these teachings are perpetuated. A lot of times the teachings are not centered on Christ but on man. It becomes about man and how his life can be filled with more money, success, and comfort and hence will become more enjoyable.

A Christ-centered approach to miracles focuses on the purpose of signs and wonders: to reveal the glory of Jesus and initiate faith in Him. In his book *Symphonic Theology* Vern Poythress says a miracle is "an extraordinary visible act of God to deliver his people and attest his word."[30]

When our focus is on Him, we are able to avoid the tendency to simply use God to get what we want. Again the writer of John said, "Jesus did many other miraculous signs in the presence of His disciples, which are not recorded in this book. But these are written that you may believe

Jesus is the Christ, the Son of God, and that by believing you may have life in His name."[31]

THE LAST VALUE

Long before malls were invented, Jesus knew where the hearts of people were: money, food, and clothes. Is it any wonder that people flock to malls? The mall is where we find the concentration of these three operating in harmony.

In the mall are all kinds of things people enjoy: food, toys, books, music, video games, movies, and so on. But interestingly, clothes, shoes, bags, jewelry, cosmetics, and other things people wear dominate malls. If money represents economics and food represents what people enjoy, what do clothes represent?

I am convinced clothes represent the variety of goods and services people value. In Jesus's hierarchy of values these fall into the lowest category but are valuable nonetheless.

The bigger picture is not that we value goods, products, and services but that we value excellence. Apart from having the right price (economics) and being enjoyable, the items people value most exude a level of excellence that warrants their consumption in the mall. People value what is economically sound, what they enjoy, and what is excellent.

It was *Good to Great* author Jim Collins and his team who correctly analyzed what the corporate world values without realizing that Jesus Christ had profoundly spoken about the same thing more than two thousand years before his team's research.

Collins called it one's "hedge-hog." He correctly pointed out that when a person is able to do what he is passionate about (or enjoys), performs the task with excellence (is the best at it), and is able to generate economic return from that work, he finds his "sweet spot" in the place where these three overlap.

A *sweet spot* is defined as "the area around the center of mass of a bat, racket, or head of a club that is the most effective part with which to hit a ball."[32] Life becomes most effective when our economics, enjoyment, and excellence come together—excellence completes the picture; it cannot be downplayed.

Once again we find the overlaps of life. We become excellent when we enjoy what we do. When we are excellent, we most likely will be paid for what we do. When we are paid, we have the resources to enjoy more. As the cycle continues, our level of excellence, economics, and enjoyment increases.

What does this have to do with discipleship? Christians must exude a level of excellence in their life and conduct. Discipleship must translate into a life of excellence. We are encouraged by Scripture to model a life of excellence:

> But just as you excel in everything—in faith, in speech, in knowledge, in complete earnestness and in your love for us—see that you also excel in this grace of giving.[33]

Paul writing to the Corinthians reminded them to be excellent "in everything"—faith, speech, knowledge, love, and even in generosity.

Mediocrity is one of the reasons the uninitiated are turned off with Christians who supposedly are "ambassadors of God," His representatives on earth. When we become doomsayers instead of hope-builders, rumormongers rather than keepers of trust, slackers when we should be models of diligence, the integrity of our faith becomes questionable.

Christianity has long been suffering under a tyranny of mediocrity. We have somehow managed to convince ourselves that as long as we perform religious rituals and make pious pronouncements, we can get by with lower quality in the other facets of life.

To excel is to be distinguishable from the rest. As we live a life of excellence, the world is left with no other alternative but to desire to know more. It's the reason we choose certain restaurants and would not be caught dead in others. Excellence causes people to take stock and notice. Excellence draws people.

This brings me to the final reason we desire and admire things or people of excellence. It is because we have been internally wired to seek and desire significance. If God is most valuable and we are what He values most, we have within our souls a longing for excellence, a desire for significance. As my good friend Greg Mitchell has said, "Denying oneself of significance is denying our God-given design. He created us with a purpose—to reflect His love and power to others. To the degree we embrace this calling is how much our lives have eternal significance."

To desire excellence and significance is not a bad thing. When we excel and do something significant we glorify God. Excellence and significance fail us when we use it to glorify ourselves and find fulfillment in it apart from God. Excellence and significance serve us as we glorify God and are satisfied with our lives in God. Excellence is valuable but not at the expense of our relationship with God and with others, or even at the expense of the health of our bodies.

THE "IRON MAN"

I met A. C. Green in 1987. The LA Lakers had just won the NBA championship against the Boston Celtics. You would think that a young man who had just won such a victory would celebrate with a cruise in the Bahamas. He didn't. Instead he went to Manila for an outreach playing exhibition games on college campuses and leading basketball clinics for young upstarts.

AC was discipled in Los Angeles and felt challenged to go on a short-term mission trip to the Philippines. I remember driving to the different campuses with the basketball superstar, his legs awkwardly folded in a cramped Asian car as he chomped on Big Macs between matches. AC was not just a great ball player; he also had an endearing air of humility.

In basketball circles AC is known as the "Iron Man." He holds the record for playing more than 1,190 consecutive games, a testimony to an amazing work ethic and the protection of God from injuries. As a Christian he excelled not just in the game but also in his lifestyle. In an industry where women throw themselves at the players, AC was a beacon of light. He came into the game as a virgin and ended his career as one. He did it not to advocate "safe sex" but because he was a disciple of Christ.

He modeled the words the apostle Paul wrote to Timothy, "Don't let anyone look down on you because you are young, but set an example for the believers in speech, in life, in love, in faith and in purity."[34]

I was recently with AC, now middle-aged and retired from the game. He has managed to stay fit and healthy. He remains a trusted ambassador of the sport and has seen success in business. AC does not hold the most glamorous of stats, nor is he a "gazillionaire," but his excellence has allowed him to reach out to others as an ambassador of Christ, whether that's in the NBA, on college campuses, in the inner cities, or even in business.

By excellence I don't mean, as the world does, that we should excel in the pursuit of being "numero uno." By excellence I mean to be set apart and distinguishable so that our lives can point people to God. This is what it means to be salt and light. Salt is distinguished by its taste and preserving qualities. Light shines. Both are distinguishable; both have value. When we lose our excellence we lose our ability to be distinguishable; we lose our value:

> You are the salt of the earth. But if the salt loses its saltiness, how can it be made salty again? It is no longer good for anything, except to be thrown out and trampled by men.[35]

According to Jesus, we become good for nothing when we lose our excellence. We get stomped by the world rather than being its preservative and the very thing that gives it flavor.

God, life, and body—these are the top-line values. Economics, enjoyment, and excellence—these represent the bottom-line values, but they are valuable nonetheless. Discipleship also means to be empowered in all six universal values of mankind.

Even after fifty years LEGO bricks do not show any signs of waning. Sales are strong and growing.[36] No doubt among the reasons for its success are LEGO's unique product proposition that brings together its patented stud and coupling system with colorful pieces that allow children to build, dismantle, and rebuild.

However, there is another thing that makes LEGO a successful product and company: the fact that it produces an economically sound product that is enjoyable and excellent. Likewise Christians should bring together their unique ability to connect to God and one another while demonstrating an ability to be economically sound, enjoyable, and excellent.

14.

PIECING IT ALL TOGETHER

I WAS IN WHITE River, South Africa, somewhere between the city of Nelspruit and Kruger National Park. I was teaching a class titled "Discipleship Is Relationship" to pastors from various parts of the continent with participants ranging from young church planters and missionaries to veteran ministers who have been in the field for many years. The class was a medley of cultures both denominationally and ethnically.

At the end of one of the sessions I noticed a couple who did not look like they were enjoying the class. I purposely walked over to them to find out if they were getting anything out of it.

I thanked them for allowing me to speak into their lives even though they had obviously been in ministry longer than I had. The woman smiled apologetically and replied, "We are overwhelmed. We've heard of discipleship but never understood it this way. Nobody told us. We've been busy with all kinds of activities but not discipleship. We don't know where to start."

My heart went out to them. It was never my intention to leave this couple feeling overwhelmed, nor is that my desire now. But I know that if this message can leave veteran ministers feeling that way, how much more Christians who have been uninvolved in discipleship?

After the workshop on values there were even more puzzled faces among the students. This time a young man approached me who at one point seemed to have many questions but now stood before me speechless. I guess he did not know where to start. I asked him how he was finding the classes. He too said, "I am overwhelmed."

I asked, "Over what?" He said, "God, relationships, health, economics, enjoyment, excellence—how can I do all of these?" I can only agree with him. When we are first confronted with the six universal values and how they play out in our everyday lives, it can be overwhelming.

I have often been asked, "How can I even remember all these things: trust, love, forgiveness, communication, plus these six values? Where do I begin? I can't even begin to picture it."

My standard answer is it is really not very hard. In fact, this is the beautiful thing about seeing everything, especially our faith, from the lenses of relationships. It's OK to be overwhelmed, but we don't have to feel bad because it isn't about being perfect. It's about staying in relationship. We are not trying to meet a quota or fulfill a set of requirements.

The more we consider it, the less pressured we become, because we have no fear of failing. At the core of this message is that we must be in relationship in order for discipleship to occur. But our first relationship is with God, and He is the one who gives us the grace to live everything else out.

He is gracious enough to forgive us for making mistakes. He is gracious enough to lead us to the truth when we are in error. And He is so gracious to give us the power to walk in the truth He has shown us.

As disciples who make disciples, we must understand that all our relationships and all that we value can only be had through the riches of God's grace. When we walk by grace, we should not, and will not, be overwhelmed.

For starters it is humanly impossible to even have a relationship with God apart from grace. J. I. Packer writes in his classic book *Knowing God*, "To mend our own relationship with God, regaining God's favour after having once lost it, is beyond the power of any one of us."[1] It is only possible by grace. "For it is by grace you have been saved, through faith—and this not from yourselves, it is the gift of God."[2]

Grace does not only start our relationship with God, but it is also what sustains it in ever increasing measure. We read in the Book of Romans, "Where sin increased, grace increased all the more, so that, just as sin reigned in death, so also grace might reign through righteousness to bring eternal life through Jesus Christ our Lord."[3]

ONLY BY GRACE

Paul writing to the Corinthians tells of a mysterious occurrence known to Bible readers as the "thorn in the flesh":

> To keep me from becoming conceited because of these surpassingly great revelations, there was given me a thorn in my flesh, a messenger of Satan, to torment me.[4]

There are a variety of speculations about what this thorn was. There are two that stand out. Some say this was a failed relationship with certain church members who endlessly pricked Paul with criticisms. Others believe the thorn was an ailment in Paul's body that stemmed from the persecution he experienced. Scripture is unclear but hints on these two as the following verse suggests:

> That is why, for Christ's sake, I delight in weaknesses, in insults, in hardships, in persecutions, in difficulties. For when I am weak, then I am strong.[5]

Whether this pertained to a relationship or an illness, Paul explains God's answer to his problem:

> But he said to me, "My grace is sufficient for you, for my power is made perfect in weakness." Therefore I will boast all the more gladly about my weaknesses, so that Christ's power may rest on me.[6]

Whether Paul's thorn was an issue involving a relationship or something about the health of his body, God's grace was sufficient. The writer of Hebrews lets us know that God's grace is *always* sufficient: "Let us then approach the throne of grace with confidence, so that we may receive mercy and find grace to help us in our time of need."[7]

Even in the area of material provision, God's grace is well able to provide for us. Notice how the grace of God provided for an entire congregation of believers by His grace.

> With great power the apostles continued to testify to the resurrection of the Lord Jesus, and much grace was upon them all. There were no needy persons among them.[8]

God's abundant grace is well able to meet us at our point of need. He can provide all the things we need at anytime we need it: "And God is able to make all grace abound to you, so that *in all things at all times*, having *all that you need*, you will abound in every good work."[9]

Radical author David Platt agrees that, "This is not a genie-in-a-bottle approach to God that assumes he is ready to grant our every wish. But it is a rock solid promise that the resources of heaven are ready and waiting for the people of God who desire to make much of him in this world."[10] It is His grace and His grace alone that will empower us to go and make disciples of all nations.

To do the work of ministry without grace is unwise. Ministry is not the work of our flesh but only works in cooperation with God and His grace. Scripture says, "And if by grace, then it is no longer by works; if it were, grace would no longer be grace."[11]

Here are two instances where ministry was accomplished not by the efforts of men but by the grace of God:

> Now Stephen, a man full of God's grace and power, did great wonders and miraculous signs among the people.[12]

> So Paul and Barnabas spent considerable time there, speaking boldly for the Lord, who confirmed the message of his grace by enabling them to do miraculous signs and wonders.[13]

I once heard Pastor James Ryle say it is God's grace that enables or empowers us to be who He has created us to be and to do what He has called us to do. Grace is the combination of God's never-ending presence and inexhaustible power that is at work every day of our lives.

It is His presence and power that we don't deserve but have been blessed and favored with. Grace was lavished upon us through the blood of Christ: "In him we have redemption through his blood, the forgiveness of sins, in accordance with the riches of God's grace that he lavished on us."[14]

The Chairman and the Thief

To fully understand grace we must distinguish what makes it different from mercy. A good but certainly not comprehensive way of understanding grace is through an illustration I call the Chairman and the Thief.

Imagine being an employee of a bank. Through the years you have figured out a way to secretly embezzle small amounts of money without being caught. Because you have gotten away with the crime for so many years, the amount you have stolen piled up into the millions. It is at this point that an audit reveals what you have been doing.

After the investigations you are called in by the chairman and presented with records proving without a doubt that you are a thief. You wait for the pronouncement of the verdict and begin imagining the dire future before you only to hear the chairman say, "Joey, I forgive you."

That's mercy—to be absolved of the punishment you deserve and the stigma that comes from being guilty of wrongdoing. Justice is when you receive the just punishment for your wrongdoing. Mercy is when you are pardoned and the punishment due you is not meted out.

As you attempt to catch your breath, you are given yet another shock when the chairman says, "You are free to go home; I forgive you."

All of this is incredible, but grace is much more. Grace is when you came to office the next day to collect your belongings and find out that the chairman has moved you up to the executive floor and made you not just the vice chairman but has offered to adopt you as his son. That's grace—when you start getting privileges you don't deserve.

When you reach the penthouse, the chairman ushers you into your new corner office. Flabbergasted by the turn of events, you don't know how to react. As you look at the new surroundings, the perks and the privileges, the chairman leads you to the glass window and points to what's happening in the street below. Just then you see the chairman's son handcuffed and being led to the police car.

Because the chairman was just and holy, he would not short-circuit the righteous process. Sin must be atoned for and paid. But because of his great love, his son offered himself as a ransom for me, the thief. This is what God has done. At great cost we have been graced by God.

The dumbest thing to do at this point is to go down to our old office and start stealing again—or worse, to steal even more because now we have the backing of the chairman. This is what we do when we flash grace as a license to sin against God and our fellow men. We have been promoted to sonship, but we choose to live like slaves.

But grace is not just access given to us by God. It is also the power to live out that relationship every day in this present life and not just in heaven: "For the grace of God that brings salvation has appeared to all men. It teaches us to say 'No' to ungodliness and worldly passions, and to live self-controlled, upright and godly lives in this present age."[15]

The right response to this grace is, "Sir, thank You for Your mercy and the grace to be Your son. What a privilege. In fact, I am so overwhelmed by Your kindness I would like to dedicate every day of my life to learning to be just like You. The fact is, I have not met anyone like You. Again, thank You very much. And may I say I love You very much too!"

Grace is not a license to wantonly sin against God. Grace is the pass card to a relationship with God.

Grace Is Also About Relationships

Some people see grace as a "force" that empowers us, or a blessing or type of favor that follows us. Grace is so much more than that. As Andy Stanley puts it, "Grace is understood best within the context of relationship. After all, it is only within the mystery and complexity of relationships that grace is experienced."[16]

Andy's book *The Grace of God* looks at God's grace from a relational perspective starting in Genesis and working its way through the Bible. His point: God's grace has been there all along. Today we can enjoy His presence and power in full measure because of our relationship with the Father that was restored to us in Christ.

> We have seen his glory, the glory of the One and Only, who came from the Father, full of grace and truth.[17]

John tells us that Jesus is the full expression of God's grace. Our daily communion with Christ is the divine assurance that we have His presence and power in our lives. And "from the fullness of his grace we have all received one blessing after another. For the law was given through Moses; grace and truth came through Jesus Christ."[18]

After all is said and done, this Christian life really is not just about grace but about a relationship with the One who is full of grace, who came and brought us grace: Jesus.

A HUNDRED-YEAR-OLD STORY

I have chosen to end this book with a hundred-year-old story of discipleship. Virginia was born in 1902. Her father, Rafael, was a member of the Palma family, a family made famous by Rafael's younger brother, Jose Palma, who was credited for writing the lyrics of the Philippine National Anthem.[19]

Rafael himself was a senator and concurrently held a cabinet position as secretary of interior in 1916, just as Virginia was becoming a teenager. As Virginia blossomed into adulthood, her father became president of the nation's leading educational institution, the University of the Philippines, and served in that position for a full decade.[20] In 1919 her mother, Carolina Ocampo, and members of Manila's socialites cofounded the Philippine Women's University, where Virginia would be educated.[21]

Virginia married a successful lawyer, who became a congressman and a member of the Philippine House of Representatives. He too would serve as a member of the cabinet of Philippine president Manuel Quezon and even become governor of his province of Laguna. Virginia would bear four children, two boys and two girls, and raise a family. Professionally she became an accomplished educator and author of textbooks on the Filipino language.

As for religion, Virginia and her husband were devout. Their home boasted its own chapel complete with pews, icons of the Stations of the Cross, an ivory crucifix, and a gold-plated tabernacle. In those days hers was a fabled life, or so it seemed.

When Virginia was in her mid-sixties, her health began to fail. She had severe hypertension, diabetes, a heart condition, and was afflicted with rheumatoid arthritis. The combined effect of all these caused her body to be wracked with pain. Pain relievers and tranquilizers became a daily part of her life. She also suffered from depression.

At age seventy-three Virginia was widowed, but loneliness was only one of her problems as her health continued to deteriorate. Strapped for cash as her remaining assets slowly dwindled to cover for her medical bills and daily sustenance, Virginia no longer had the celebrated life she once knew.

She naturally turned to her religion but could not find solace in it. She turned to New Age seminars and came out empty. She even tried to just be an intellectual humanist, but even that didn't help. She had become distraught, ornery, and desperate.

In 1979 she was invited to a church service. At this meeting Virginia finally came to her senses and realized that only Jesus could give her the life she needed and wanted. By the grace of God at the age of seventy-seven she became a follower of Christ.

Acknowledging her sinful nature and need for a Savior, she gave her life to Jesus, put her faith in Him, and became His disciple. At eighty-three she wrote a booklet titled *Fruitfulness in Old Age*. In it she shares of her repentance, faith, and baptism in Christ and the Holy Spirit. She also writes of the opportunities God gave her to share the gospel of Jesus Christ with others as she lived an empowered life every day.

She wrote: "Going out for the first time to share the good news of Christ's free gift of salvation was an exciting and thrilling experience for a newcomer like me. I met all kinds of people. I saw both rich and poor transformed by God's Holy Spirit."[22]

She shared her newfound relationship with Jesus with her family, relatives, and friends. At first members of her family thought old age, depression, and desperation had gotten the better of her. But her transformation was uncanny—she changed right before their eyes. Even her physical health and personal finances were transformed supernaturally. God's grace simply empowered her.

Over time the fruit of her life in Christ proved itself to be true. One by one members of her family also became followers of Jesus.

EXTENDING GRACE TO OTHERS

On one of her properties Virginia had a tin-roofed wooden shack built, which she used to reach out to the poor with the little money she had left. Being an educator, she taught the mothers and young women in the community to teach their children to read. She naturally shared her faith as she interacted with them. On weekends she invited pastors from her church to share the Word of God with them. Eventually the services at her shack began to grow, and many came to Christ.

Well into her eighties, Virginia also shared her faith with the elderly who were downtrodden. Again in her pamphlet she writes of how the Holy Spirit empowered her:

> Many of these elders were found in the streets. They left home for nobody cared for them. They have become useless according to the world. I shared my life to them, how the Lord carried me as He promised. I told them how I stood by the promise of God and not to lose heart nor give up.
>
> The Holy Spirit carried the Lord's message of love that touched their hearts, according to their own testimonies. We lavished them with food, biscuits, blankets and more things that they needed. The experience was something uplifting.[23]

As a disciple of Christ, Virginia realized a fundamental truth about grace: it is meant to be shared with others. The promise of prosperity and power that comes by grace is nothing compared to the pleasure of seeing others experience and enjoy God's grace.

In 1996, seventeen years after Virginia became a follower of Christ, a pastor visited her at the hospital. At age ninety-four she was nearing the end of her life on earth. She turned to the young pastor and said, "Don't pray for my healing. I have already talked to Jesus. I'm going home." The next day she died.

I know this firsthand. I was that young pastor. You see, Virginia is my father's mother.

My grandmother Virginia is the one who first engaged me about Jesus when I was a teenager. Though I constantly rejected her message about Christ, she continually prayed that I would one day encounter His grace and give my life to Him. It was also by watching her life that I saw what it meant to repent, have faith, and be baptized. She modeled how to co-labor with Christ as His disciple while living life each day.

Apart from attending Bible studies and having sound theology, her life embodied the top-tier values of God and life. This even translated into the inexplicable healing of her body at one point and the supernatural provision of her needs. Once a depressed woman she was transformed into one who exuded joy that was undeniable. In faith, in speech, in knowledge, in love, and even in generosity she excelled.

In her dying moments, she demonstrated what it is like to be certain of one's eternal home and to glorify God with one's life.

AN ETERNAL LEGACY

In the years of her greatest weakness and need, my grandmother Virginia gave us, her descendants, the greatest gift of all: Jesus. Her life was a testimony to the presence, power, and love of God—in her we saw the workings of His amazing grace.

Today my father, mother, siblings, wife, and children have become followers of Jesus. From Virginia have come four generations of disciples. This is a picture of an empowered disciple-maker. In the eyes of the world she became a poor, weak, sick old woman. In the eyes of God she passed on to her descendants the richest inheritance of all.

Everyone—man, woman, young, old, rich, poor—should be a disciple who makes disciples. This is the hope of the nations and the way to transform the world one person at a time. To this mission Jesus promised we would be empowered, saying, "Surely I am with you always, to the very end of the age."[24]

LEGO bricks are built to connect multigenerationally. That means bricks made back in the 1950s connect just as well with those made in 2012. Connecting them is not a problem. Likewise, when people make disciples through relationships, generational, traditional, and denominational differences fall by the wayside.

And just as LEGO pieces come from different boxes, so can Christians from different streams and denominations connect together to reach the world for Jesus. With the right building blocks and values, we can connect people to Christ and to one another.

Like LEGO that connect brick by brick, discipleship is about connecting the world to a relationship with Christ one person at a time. This we do as we engage, establish, equip, and empower people.

NOTES

INTRODUCTION

1. Mark 12:30–31.

1. JUST LIKE LEGO

1. Christian Humberg, *50 Years of the LEGO Brick* (n.p.: Heel Verlag Gmbh, 2008), 9
2. Ibid., 9.
3. Jonathan Bender, *LEGO: A Love Story* (Hoboken, NJ: John Wiley & Sons, Inc., 2010), 50.
4. Daniel Lipkowitz, *The LEGO Book: The Amazing LEGO Story* (New York: DK Publishing, 2009), 12.
5. Bender, *LEGO: A Love Story*, 50.
6. David Pickering, Nick Turpin, and Caryn Jenner, *The Ultimate LEGO Book* (New York: DK Publishing, 1999), 10.
7. Humberg, *50 Years of the LEGO Brick*, 11.
8. Ibid.
9. Pickering, Turpin, and Jenner, *The Ultimate LEGO Book*, 10.
10. Ibid.
11. Ibid., 12.
12. Bender, *LEGO: A Love Story*, 50.
13. Matthew 22:37–38.
14. Matthew 22:39.
15. Bill Hull, *The Complete Book of Discipleship* (Colorado Springs, CO: NavPress, 2006), 35.
16. Matthew 28:19–20, emphasis added.
17. Matthew 3:16–17.
18. Rick Warren, *The Purpose Driven Life* (Grand Rapids, MI: Zondervan, 2002), 117.
19. David Platt, *Radical* (Colorado Springs, CO: Multnomah, 2010), 93.
20. Matthew 28:20.
21. John 14:15.
22. John 15:17.
23. John 15:14.
24. John 13:35.
25. John 5:39–40.
26. John Telford, ed., *The Letters of John Wesley* (London: Epworth Press, 1931), Letter to Joseph Benson, November 7, 1768.
27. John 21:17.
28. John 21:17.

29. 1 John 4:19.
30. 1 Corinthians 8:1.
31. 1 Corinthians 12:31.
32. 1 Corinthians 13:13.
33. Ted Engstrom, *The Making of a Christian Leader* (Grand Rapids, MI: Zondervan, 1976), 81.
34. 2 Corinthians 5:18–19.
35. 1 Corinthians 4:14.
36. 1 Corinthians 4:16.
37. Francis Frangipane, *When the Many Are One* (Lake Mary, FL: Charisma House, 2009), 111.
38. 1 Corinthians 11:23–25.
39. Jane Macartney, "One Billion Souls to Save," *The Times*, March 28, 2009.
40. Verna Yu, *Sunday Morning Post*, May 8, 2011, 13.
41. Andy Stanley and Bill Willits, *Creating Community* (Colorado Springs, CO: Multnomah, 2004), 63–64.

2. In One Word

1. Thom Rainer and Eric Geiger, *Simple Church* (Nashville, TN: B & H Publishing, 2006), 19.
2. Ibid., 16.
3. See Acts 4:13.
4. Matthew 28:19–20.
5. See Matthew 1:21.
6. See Acts 1:8.
7. Acts 10:3–7.
8. LeRoy Eims, *The Lost Art of Making Disciples* (Grand Rapids, MI: Zondervan, 1978), 55–56.
9. From a class Jun Escosar taught at Victory's School of World Missions in June 1995.
10. Albert Winseman, *Growing an Engaged Church* (New York: Gallup Press, 2006), 3–5.
11. Ibid., 5.
12. Ibid.
13. The Barna Group, Pew Forum on Religion and Public Life, "What's Going Wrong?", *Ministry Today*, September/October 2009, 38.
14. Hull, *The Complete Book of Discipleship*, 118.
15. W. Vaus, *Mere Theology* (Downers Grove, IL: InterVarsity Press, 2004), 167.
16. Ibid.
17. Hull, *The Complete Book of Discipleship*, 118.

18. Howard Schultz, *Pour Your Heart Into It* (New York: Hyperion, 1997), 25–26.
19. *New Oxford American Dictionary*, s.v. "lego," http://oxforddictionaries .com/definition/Lego (accessed June 19, 2012).

3. Discipleship Is Relationship

1. See Isaiah 40:28.
2. Henry T. Blackaby and Richard Blackaby, *Experiencing God Day by Day* (Nashville, TN: B&H Publishing Group, 2006), 131.
3. John Piper, *The Dangerous Duty of Delight* (Colorado Springs, CO: Multnomah Publishers, 2001).
4. Amby Burfoot, *Complete Running Book* (Emmaus, PA: Rodale Inc., 2004), 290, 292
5. Luke 9:23.
6. John 16:33.
7. 1 Peter 4:13.
8. John Piper, *Desiring God* (Colorado Springs, CO: Multnomah, 2003), 288.
9. James 1:2–3.
10. Romans 5:3–4.
11. Romans 8:17.
12. C. S. Lewis, *The Problem of Pain* (New York, NY: HarperCollins, 2001), 5.
13. Acts 5:41.
14. Genesis 2:18.
15. Piper, *Desiring God*, 288.
16. *Merriam-Webster Online Dictionary*, s.v. "agenda," http://www.merriam -webster.com/dictionary/agenda?show=0&t=1337203126 (accessed May 16, 2012).
17. Ed Stetzer and David Putnam, *Breaking the Missional Code* (Nashville, TN: Broadman & Holman Publishers, 2006), 82.
18. See Luke 15:12.
19. See Luke 15:17–18.
20. Luke 15:16, emphasis added.
21. Luke 15:17, emphasis added.
22. Luke 15:18.
23. See John 16:8.
24. See John 3:5–6.
25. Luke 15:20.
26. Luke 15:22–24.
27. See Isaiah 61:10.
28. See Genesis 41:42.
29. See Mark 1:7.
30. Luke 15:28.

31. Luke 15:29.
32. Luke 15:30.
33. Dallas Willard, *The Spirit of the Disciplines* (New York: HarperCollins, 1988), 138.
34. Luke 15:31–32.
35. Martin Luther, *Address to the Christian Nobility of the German Nation Respecting the Reformation of the Christian Estate,* XXXVI, Part 5, The Harvard Classics (New York: P. F. Collier & Son, 1909–1914), Bartleby .com, 2001, http://www.bartleby.com/36/5/ (accessed May 15, 2012).

4. Building Blocks

1. Larry Osborne, *Spirituality for the Rest of Us* (Colorado Springs, CO: Multnomah, 2009).
2. Ibid.
3. Genesis 1:26, emphasis added.
4. Psalm 8:4, 6.
5. Genesis 2:16–17.
6. See Genesis 3:8.
7. Genesis 3:9.
8. Genesis 3:10.
9. Genesis 3:11, emphasis added.
10. Genesis 3:11.
11. See Genesis 3:4–5.
12. Genesis 3:12, emphasis added.
13. See Genesis 1:27.
14. C. S. Lewis, *God in the Dock* (Grand Rapids, MI: Wm. B. Eerdmans Publishing Co., 1994).
15. Genesis 3:13.
16. Genesis 3:6.
17. James 1:13–14, emphasis added.
18. Genesis 3:16–17, emphasis added.
19. Lewis, *The Problem of Pain*, 91.
20. Genesis 3:18–19.
21. See Genesis 2:16.
22. Dudley Hall, *Grace Works* (Ann Arbor, MI: Servant Publications, 1992), 182.
23. See Isaiah 14:12–14.
24. Andrew Murray, *Humility* (Bloomington, MN: Bethany House Publishers, 2001), 18.
25. Genesis 3:20.
26. John King, trans., *Calvin's Commentaries: Genesis, Part I* (n.p.: Forgotten Books, 2007), 116.

27. Genesis 2:23.
28. Genesis 3:21.
29. Abridged by Ralph Earle, *Adam Clarke's Commentary on the Bible* (Nashville, TN: Thomas Nelson Incorporated, 1997).
30. *Zondervan NIV Bible Commentary* (Grand Rapids, MI: Zondervan Publishing House, 1994), 11.
31. Noah Webster, *American Dictionary of the English Language* (Chesapeake, VA: Foundation for American Christian Education, 1968), s.v. "atonement."
32. J. I. Packer, *Knowing God Through the Year* (Downers Grover, IL: Inter-Varsity Press, 2004), 101.
33. John 1:29.
34. Tim Keller, *The Reason for God* (New York: Dutton, 2008), 191.
35. Matthew 5:45.
36. Paul B. Caroll and Chunka Mui, *Billion Dollar Lessons* (New York: Penguin, 2008), 15.
37. Genesis 3:24.
38. Genesis 5:5.
39. Genesis 5:3–4, emphasis added.
40. Genesis 4:1, emphasis added.
41. Genesis 5:8.
42. Genesis 5:11.
43. Genesis 5:23-24.
44. Hebrews 11:5, emphasis added.

5. TRUST

1. 1 John 1:5.
2. John 1:14.
3. Rick Rusaw and Eric Swanson, *The Externally Focused Church* (Loveland, CO: Group Publishing, 2004), 11-12.
4. John 14:6, emphasis added.
5. John 16:13.
6. Ibid.
7. Psalm 51:6.
8. Numbers 23:19.
9. Luke 1:37, ASV.
10. Joshua 21:45.
11. See Hebrews 10:23.
12. Genesis 8:22.
13. Matthew 5:37.
14. 2 Corinthians 1:20.
15. 1 Corinthians 15:46.

16. See James 1:17.
17. See James 2:17.
18. 1 Chronicles 29:17.
19. Mark 1:22.
20. R. C. Sproul, *The Holiness of God* (Carol Stream, IL: Tyndale House Publishers, 1998), 37–38.
21. As quoted in J. I. Packer, *Rediscovering Holiness* (Nottingham: Crossway Books, 1992), 18.
22. Hebrews 12:14.
23. 1 Peter 1:15–16, emphasis added.
24. Ephesians 1:4, emphasis added.
25. Genesis 2:3, emphasis added.
26. Matthew 5:16.
27. Hebrews 13:8.
28. Brennan Manning, *The Ragamuffin Gospel* (Colorado Springs, CO: Multnomah Publishers, 2005), 120.

6. LOVE

1. Oswald Chambers, *My Utmost for His Highest* (Uhrichsville, OH: Barbour Publishing, Inc., 1963), 132.
2. 1 John 4:8.
3. William Girao, *The God We Have Forgotten* (Metro Manila, Philippines: OMF Literature, 2003), 127.
4. Wayne Grudem, *Systematic Theology* (Downers Grove, IL: InterVarsity, 1994), 231.
5. Genesis 1:28, emphasis added.
6. Galatians 5:22–23, emphasis added.
7. Galatians 5:19, emphasis added.
8. Martin Luther, *Commentary on the Epistle to the Galatians* (Whitefish, MT: Kessinger Publishing, 2004).
9. John 15:4–5, emphasis added.
10. John 15:8, emphasis added.
11. John 15:9, emphasis added.
12. John 13:35.
13. Romans 5:8, emphasis added.
14. See Genesis 6:13.
15. See Exodus 19:20–23.
16. See Isaiah 6:1–5.
17. See 2 Timothy 4:1.
18. Kevin J. Conner, *The Foundations of Christian Doctrine* (Portland, OR: City Christian Publishing, 1995).
19. Keller, *The Reason for God*, 197.

20. See 1 Corinthians 1:17.
21. Keller, *The Reason for God*.
22. Galatians 3:16.
23. See John 3:30.
24. Pickering, Turpin, and Jenner, *The Ultimate LEGO Book*, 9.
25. Robert Coleman, *The Master Plan of Evangelism* (OMF Literature, 1993).
26. Ibid.

7. FORGIVENESS

1. Matthew 5:48.
2. Matthew 5:44–46.
3. Lamentations 3:22–23, ESV.
4. St. Augustine, *De Trinitate*, vol. I, 10, 12.
5. Psalm 19:1–2.
6. Luke Tyerman, *Life and Times of the Rev. John Wesley, M. A., Founder of the Methodists* (London: Hodder and Stoughton, 1876), 451.
7. Psalm 89:14.
8. James 2:13.
9. John Paul II, *Centesimus Annus* (1991), item 25, paragraph 3, http://tinyurl.com/5m32e (accessed May 15, 2012).
10. James 1:15.
11. Genesis 4:3–5.
12. Hebrews 11:4.
13. Hebrews 11:4.
14. Genesis 4:6–7.
15. Genesis 4:7.
16. Romans 7:19–20.
17. Deuteronomy 5:17.
18. Keller, *The Reason for God*, 170–171.
19. Lewis B. Smedes, *Forgive and Forget: Healing the Hurts We Don't Deserve* (New York: HarperCollins, 1996), 67.
20. Romans 4:7.
21. Isaiah 55:7.
22. Genesis 4:9–10.
23. Genesis 4:13, emphasis added.
24. Francis Chan, *Crazy Love* (Colorado Springs, CO: David C. Cook, 2008), 86.
25. Genesis 4:11–12, emphasis added.
26. Matthew 11:28–29, emphasis added.
27. Romans 12:1, emphasis added.
28. 1 Corinthians 13:7.
29. 1 Corinthians 13:5.

30. Romans 3:25, NIV (1978).
31. Revelation 1:5, emphasis added.
32. Matthew 26:28, emphasis added.
33. Romans 8:28, KJV.
34. Smedes, *Forgive and Forget: Healing the Hurts We Don't Deserve.*

8. COMMUNICATION

1. Genesis 3:1, emphasis added.
2. Genesis 2:16, emphasis added.
3. Genesis 3:1, emphasis added.
4. Genesis 3:2–3.
5. Proverbs 30:5.
6. See Proverbs 30:6; Revelation 22:18–19.
7. Genesis 3:4–5.
8. Genesis 3:6.
9. Genesis 3:7–8, emphasis added.
10. Richard J. Foster, *Celebration of Discipline* (San Francisco, CA: Harper-SanFrancisco, 1998), 17.
11. Edwin Louis Cole, *Communication, Sex and Money,* (Tulsa, OK: Harrison House, Inc., 1987), 23.
12. Daniel Henderson with Margaret Saylar, *Fresh Encounters* (Colorado Springs, CO: NavPress, 2008).
13. Russ Busby, *Billy Graham, God's Ambassador* (San Diego: Tehabi Books, 1999), 25.
14. Ibid.
15. Derek Prince, *Foundation Series* (Lancaster, England: Sovereign World, 1986), 27.
16. *New Living Translation* (Wheaton, IL: Tyndale House Publishers, Inc., 2007).
17. Henderson and Saylar, *Fresh Encounters.*
18. Hull, *The Complete Book of Discipleship*, 91.
19. Ibid.
20. James 1:19, emphasis added.
21. Robert Logan and Sherilyn Carlton, *Coaching 101* (Saint Charles, IL: ChurchSmart Resources, 2003), 33.
22. Henderson and Saylar, *Fresh Encounters*, 74.
23. 1 John 3:18.
24. Hull, *The Complete Book of Discipleship*, 157.
25. UIS Fact Sheet, "Adult and Youth Literacy," UNESCO Institute for Statistics, September 2011, No. 16, http://www.uis.unesco.org/FactSheets/Documents/FS16-2011-Literacy-EN.pdf (accessed April 16, 2012).
26. See Romans 14:17.

27. John Ortberg, *The Life You've Always Wanted* (Grand Rapids, MI: Zondervan, 1997), 51.
28. John 3:8.
29. Hebrews 12:24.
30. Mark 4:28.
31. Christian A. Schwarz, *Natural Church Development* (Saint Charles, IL: ChurchSmart Resources, 1996), 12.
32. Luke 6:45.

9. Brick by Brick

1. Bender, *LEGO: A Love Story*, 195.
2. Matthew 6:21, emphasis added.
3. See Luke 16:1–7.
4. Luke 16:8, emphasis added.
5. Luke 16:3–4.
6. Luke 16:5–7, emphasis added.
7. Luke 16:8, emphasis added.
8. Luke 16:9, emphasis added.
9. Luke 16:10.
10. Luke 16:11.
11. Luke 16:14.
12. Luke 16:15, emphasis added.
13. Matthew 6:24.
14. Matthew 26:14–15.
15. Matthew 6:19.
16. Matthew 6:20, emphasis added.
17. Francis Schaeffer, *The Mark of the Christian* (Downers Grove, IL: Inter-Varsity Press, 1978), 8–9.
18. Matthew 18:12, emphasis added.
19. Matthew 18:13, emphasis added.
20. Matthew 18:14, emphasis added.
21. Luke 10:2.
22. Aubrey Malphurs, *Advanced Strategic Planning* (Grand Rapids, MI: Baker Publishing, 2005), 101.
23. James Collins, Jerry Porras, *Built to Last* (New York: HarperCollins, 2002), 76.

10. People Are Valuable

1. Psalm 139:14.
2. Tony Buzan, *The Mind Map Book* (New York: Plume, 1996), 27.
3. Mark 8:37.

4. David Kinnaman and Gabe Lyons, *unChristian* (Grand Rapids, MI: Baker Books, 2007), 24, 27.

5. Ibid., 26.

6. Stetzer and Putnam, *Breaking the Missional Code*, 86.

7. Ibid.

8. Steve Murrell, *One2One* (Taguig City, Phillipines: Every Nation Publications, n.d.), http://www.everynationstore.com/collections/books/products/copy-of-one-to-one (accessed May 16, 2012).

9. Lawson Lau, *The World at Your Doorstep* (Downers Grove, IL: Intervarsity, 1984), 81.

10. Mark Dever, *The Gospel and Personal Evangelism* (Wheaton, IL: Crossway Books, 2007), 70–71.

11. Bill Hybels, *Just Walk Across the Room* (Grand Rapids, MI: Zondervan, 2006), 41.

12. John 4:37–38.

13. 1 Corinthians 3:6–7.

14. Pickering, Turpin, and Jenner, *The Ultimate LEGO Book*, 17.

15. Mark Driscoll, *Confessions of a Reformission Rev* (Grand Rapids, MI: Zondervan, 2006), 94.

11. Jesus Is Most Valuable

1. Mark 14:33–34.

2. Mark 14:35–36.

3. See Hebrews 11:19.

4. Matthew 7:25.

5. 1 Timothy 6:17, emphasis added.

6. 1 Timothy 6:19, emphasis added.

7. Rice Broocks and Steve Murrell, *The Purple Book* (Grand Rapids, MI: Zondervan, 2004), 10.

8. 1 Corinthians 3:11, emphasis added.

9. See Ephesians 2:19–20.

10. Hebrews 6:1–2, emphasis added.

11. Matthew 4:17.

12. See Matthew 26:28.

13. See John 1:12–13.

14. See 2 Corinthians 1:20–22.

15. See Philippians 4:13.

16. See Philippians 4:19.

17. See Romans 8:37.

18. See Galatians 3:13.

19. See Hebrews 10:19.

20. See Romans 6:23.

21. See Ephesians 1:3.
22. See Philippians 3:9.
23. See Philippians 4:7.
24. See Ephesians 2:6.
25. See Romans 8:39.
26. See 1 John 5:4.
27. See Romans 6:4.
28. See Acts 2:41.
29. See Colossians 2:11–12.
30. See Mark 1:41.
31. See James 5:14–15.
32. See Acts 9:17.
33. See 1 Timothy 4:14.
34. See Mark 16:17–18.
35. See 2 Corinthians 6:1.
36. See Luke 10:17.
37. See John 11:25.
38. Acts 24:15.
39. Acts 24:16.
40. See 1 Corinthians 15:42–44.
41. Proverbs 14:32.
42. See 1 Thessalonians 2:19.
43. See 2 Timothy 2:5.
44. See 2 Timothy 4:8.
45. See 1 Peter 5:4.
46. See Revelation 2:10.
47. Revelation 4:10–11.
48. See Genesis 15:1.
49. "Holy, Holy, Holy" by Reginald Heber. Public domain.
50. See John 1:1–3.
51. Greg Ogden, *The New Reformation* (Grand Rapids, MI: Zondervan, 1991), 109.
52. 1 Timothy 3:14–15, emphasis added.
53. 1 Corinthians 12:27–28.
54. See Ephesians 3:10.
55. See Matthew 16:18.
56. See Acts 25:24.
57. See Genesis 28:3.
58. See 1 Corinthians 11:18.
59. See John 17:15–21.
60. David Watson, *I Believe in the Church* (London: Hodder and Stoughton, 1978), 334.

61. Ibid., 335.
62. Bryan Chappel, *Christ-Centered Preaching* (Grand Rapids, MI: Baker Academic, 2005), 19.
63. Colossians 2:8–10.
64. Pickering, Turpin, and Jenner, *The Ultimate LEGO Book*, 12.
65. Ibid., 13.
66. Ibid.
67. Dietrich Bonhoeffer, *The Cost of Discipleship* (New York: Touchstone, 1995), 173.

12. Ministry Is Valuable

1. Elton Trueblood, *The Best of Elton Trueblood*, edited by J. R. Newby, (n.p.: Impact Books, 1979), 34.
2. Ibid.
3. Paul Becker, Jim Carpenter, and Mark Williams, *The New Dynamic Church Planting Handbook* (Oceanside, CA: Dynamic Church Planting International, 2003), 38.
4. Matthew 4:18, emphasis added.
5. Matthew 4:19.
6. Steve Addison, *Movements That Changed the World* (Downers Grove, IL: InterVarsity Press, 2011), 72–74.
7. Mark 1:16.
8. Luke 5:4, emphasis added.
9. Luke 5:6–7, emphasis added.
10. Regi Campbell with Richard Chancy, *Mentor Like Jesus* (Nashville, TN: B&H Publishing Group, 2009), 52–53.
11. Elisabeth Elliot, *Discipline: The Glad Surrender* (Grand Rapids, MI: Revell, 2006), 15.
12. Addison, *Movements That Changed the World*.
13. Foster, *Celebration of Discipline*, 9.
14. 2 Timothy 1:7.
15. Ortberg, *The Life You've Always Wanted*, 55.
16. Luke 17:10, emphasis added.
17. Ephesians 4:11–12, emphasis added.
18. Ephesians 4:12–13.

13. Every Day Is Valuable

1. Matthew 6:21.
2. Matthew 6:24, emphasis added.
3. Matthew 6:25, emphasis added.
4. Jared Diamond, *Collapse* (New York: Penguin Books, 2005), 16.

5. Ecclesiastes 9:4.
6. Diamond, *Collapse*, 16.
7. Ravi Zacharias, *Jesus Among the Gods* (Word Publishing, 2000), 68-69.
8. 1 Timothy 4:8.
9. 3 John 2.
10. Matthew 6:26.
11. Romans 5:8.
12. Romans 8:32.
13. Stetzer and Putnam, *Breaking the Missional Code*, 120.
14. Acts 1:4–5.
15. Acts 1:8.
16. See Romans 8:14, 16.
17. See John 14:26.
18. See Mark 13:11.
19. See Romans 8:26.
20. Ecclesiastes 10:19.
21. 1 Timothy 6:9.
22. 1 Timothy 6:10.
23. Howard Dayton, *Your Money Counts* (Carol Stream, IL: Tyndale House Publishers, 1997), 2.
24. Dave Ramsey, *Financial Peace Revisited* (New York: Viking/Penguin Group, 2003), 13.
25. Franky Schaeffer, ed., *Is Capitalism Christian?* (Westchester, IL: Crossway Books, 1985), xxvii.
26. Philippians 4:19, emphasis added.
27. G. K. Chesterton, *The Innocence of Father Brown* (Sioux Falls, SD: NuVision Publications, LLC, 2008), 9.
28. John 4:53.
29. Ephesians 3:20, emphasis added.
30. Vern Poythress, *Symphonic Theology* (Phillipsburg, NJ: P&R Publishing, 2001).
31. John 20:30–31.
32. *Merriam-Webster Online Dictionary*, s.v. "sweet spot," http://www.merriam-webster.com/dictionary/sweet%20spot (accessed May 16, 2012).
33. 2 Corinthians 8:7.
34. 1 Timothy 4:12.
35. Matthew 5:13.
36. "LEGO Group Sales Up by 17% in 2011," LEGO Group, March 1, 2012, http://aboutus.lego.com/en-us/news-room/2012/march/annual-result-2011/ (accessed April 18, 2012).

14. Piecing It Together

1. J. I. Packer, *Knowing God* (Downers Grover, IL: InterVarsity Press, 1973), 146.
2. Ephesians 2:8.
3. Romans 5:20–21.
4. 2 Corinthians 12:7.
5. 2 Corinthians 12:10.
6. 2 Corinthians 12:9.
7. Hebrews 4:16.
8. Acts 4:33–34.
9. 2 Corinthians 9:8, emphasis added.
10. Platt, *Radical*, 59.
11. Romans 11:6.
12. Acts 6:8.
13. Acts 14:3.
14. Ephesians 1:7–8.
15. Titus 2:11–12.
16. Andy Stanley, *The Grace of God* (Nashville, TN: Thomas Nelson, 2010).
17. John 1:14.
18. John 1:16–17.
19. *Rafael Palma: a Commemorative Brochure on His Birth Centenary* (n.p.: University of the Philippines Press, 1974), 9.
20. Parangal Sentenyal Unibersidad ng Pilipinas (n.p.: University of the Philippines Press, 2008), 16.
21. The Philippine Women's University, "About PWU," http://www.pwu.edu.ph/about/pwu-history.html (accessed May 16, 2012).
22. Virginia Palma Bonifacio, *Fruitfulness in Old Age (n.p.: n.p.,* 1982).
23. Ibid.
24. Matthew 28:20.

ACKNOWLEDGMENTS

N O DOUBT MUCH of this book has been culled from years of information and experiences from teachers, friends, associates, and other writers who are simply too many to acknowledge and thank individually. There are, however, a few who need special mention.

This book would not have been possible if not for the encouragement, support, and help of the following people:

The Early Believers

John Rohrer for prophesying. Lynn Keesecker for being an early sounding board. Keith Danby for seeing the possibility. Alex Castillo, Elias Dantas, Diame and Bianca Dumaup, Carol Lozano, Stephen Mansfield, William Murrell, and Lynn Nawata for reading the early version and giving your valuable input and encouragement.

The People of Victory

Manny Carlos, Ferdie Cabiling, Jun Escosar, Juray Mora together with the pastors and leaders of Victory, for your unending friendship, love and passion for making disciples. Much of this book comes from lessons I have learned from our collective experiences. I am always grateful to all of you for allowing me to be a part of the team.

The Theologians

Paul Barker for challenging my thoughts and generously giving yours. Jun Divierte and Winston Reyes for all your inputs and insights.

The People of Charisma

Steve Strang for trusting your instincts. Tessie DeVore for believing and orchestrating behind the scenes. Barbara Dycus for your excellence. Jevon Bolden and your outstanding team for your editorial work. Woodley Auguste and your dynamic team for the cover design and copy.

My Staff

Paolo Punzalan for taking charge so I can write. Crickette Abello and Mayet Lempin for making sure my ministry world makes sense; every pastor in the world should be blessed with amazing people like you. To the rest of the staff at Victory Fort Bonifacio—you are an amazing bunch.

My Mentors

Steve and Deborah Murrell for investing your life into mine and countless others and showing all of us that discipleship is relationship.

My Family

Marie, Joseph, David, and Joshua, for reading, rereading, sharing your thoughts, editing, and praying ceaselessly for this book. You are my first and will be my last small group on earth.

My Parents

Peping and Tina Bonifacio, your life and example will always be remembered and cherished. Thank you for being this author's first and earliest believers.